UNNECESSARY EVIL

SUNY series in Philosophy
George R. Lucas Jr., Editor

Unnecessary Evil

HISTORY AND MORAL PROGRESS
IN THE PHILOSOPHY OF
IMMANUEL KANT

SHARON ANDERSON-GOLD

State University of New York Press

Published by
State University of New York Press

© 2001 State University of New York

For information, address the State University of New York Press,
90 State Street, Suite 700, Albany, NY 12207

Marketing by Michael Campochiaro • Production by Bernadine Dawes

Library of Congress Cataloging–in–Publication Data

Anderson–Gold, Sharon, 1947–
  Unnecessary evil : history and moral progress in the philosophy of Immanuel Kant /
Sharon Anderson-Gold.
     p.   cm. – (SUNY series in philosophy)
  Includes bibliographical references and index.
  ISBN 0–7914–4819–3 (alk. paper) – ISBN 0–7914–4820–7 (pbk. : alk. paper)
    1. Kant, Immanuel, 1724–1804–Ethics. 2. Ethics. 3. Kant, Immanuel,
1724–1804–Contributions in the philosophy of history. 4. History–Philosophy. I. Title.
II Series.

B2799.E8 .A63 2001
170'.92–dc21

                                                                00–032953

1   2   3   4   5   6   7   8   9   10

to my sons jason and jordan,
who inspire all my work

Contents

Acknowledgments

I thank the following publishers for permission to republish parts of essays that appear in this book.

"God and Community: An Investigation into the Religious Implications of the Highest Good," in *Kant's Philosophy of Religion Reconsidered,* edited by Philip J. Rossi and Michael Wreen (Bloomington and Indianapolis: Indiana University Press, 1991), pp. 113–31.

"Kant's Ethical Anthropology and the Critical Foundations of Kant's Philosophy of History," *History of Philosophy Quarterly* (Tulane University), 1994, pp. 405–19.

"Crimes against Humanity: A Kantian Perspective on International Law," in *Autonomy and Community,* edited by Jane Kneller and Sidney Axnin (Albany: State University of New York Press, 1998), pp. 103–17.

"Cosmopolitanism and Cultural Pluralism," *Social Philosophy Today* 15 (forthcoming).

Preface

I have been told that this book is really two books: a book on evil and a book on history. But they are connected and I can't figure out how to separate them. My belief that moral evil and historical development are deeply connected in Kant's philosophy began with my dissertation "Teleology and Radical Evil," completed in 1980. In the conclusion of this study of Kant's concept of a "species character" I considered Silber's claim that radical evil is too "rationalistic" and cannot account for extraordinary or devilish acts. I argued that radical evil had great explanatory value once one acknowledged the role of the social context within which the principles of selfishness operate. As a result of this analysis I became quite convinced that Kant's claim that evil was the "character of the species" was itself foundational for the way in which the moral life of the individual should be understood. Traditional interpretations of evil had begun with a focus on the disposition of the individual and had ignored the social dimensions of Kant's analysis. In later publications I investigated the role that Kant assigns to the ethical commonwealth in the overcoming of evil. These analyses strengthened my perspective on the collective character of moral life.

There has been little attention, however, paid to Kant's conception of radical evil in the literature. Fackenheim had laid a foundation for the neglect of Kant's conception of evil and his conception of history by suggesting that both involved assumptions that violated Kant's ethical theory. Radical evil had long been an embarrassment to liberal ethical theorists who viewed this notion as simultaneously too pessimistic and

too religious. In fact, Fackenheim reports that Goethe was outraged
when he first read Kant's *Religion* because it appeared to be a betrayal
of the conception of autonomy central to the previously published
Groundwork. At the same time that Kant articulated this darker side of
freedom, he was developing a view of moral progress in history that
suggested that in fact human beings could and would improve their
world beyond anything his Enlightenment critics yet imagined. So here
we have two elements of Kant's system, radical evil and moral progress,
that seemed incompatible with each other and with Kant's core ethical
theory.

It is apparent to me that the real conflict among the elements of
Kant's practical philosophy stems from the "individualistic" reading of
the "core" ethical theory and his conception of radical evil. Once I
viewed the problem of evil from the perspective of the species, the
picture/puzzle looked very different. If virtue and vice are viewed as
collective tasks and are set within a context of historical development
from which individual duties in the promotion of these tasks are derived, the picture begins to take shape in a more coherent fashion.

Following the publication of William Galston's *Kant and the Problem
of History* in 1975 and Yirmiahu Yovel's *Kant and the Philosophy of History* in
1980, interest in the question of progress in history revived. This in
turn generated some additional attention to the significance of radical
evil even if only from the perspective of the barriers that it creates for
genuine moral progress. However, the connection between moral evil
and historical progress in Kant's philosophy has not, in my opinion,
been fully developed. Although not the major focus of the work, the
social context of evil was foregrounded in Alan Wood's *Kant's Moral
Religion* (1970). Yet it was not until 1990 that the first book–length study
on Kant's conception of radical evil, Gordon Michalson Jr.'s *Fallen Freedom*, appeared in English. In this work Michalson provides a very nu-
anced analysis of the complex terminology developed in the *Religion*
to deal with the relationship between freedom and evil. In his treatment evil is seen as primarily a characteristic of individual dispositions, and he makes only a passing reference to the implications of the
ethical commonwealth for a more socially oriented interpretation of
moral evil. Kant's "story" of moral progress in history is thus still seen
as operating on a different level than his ethics.

The primary purpose of this book is to integrate Kant's view of
moral evil with his views on moral progress in history. Thus two books
become one. In the process I will further develop the role of reflective
judgment in the interpretation of history articulated in Rudolf Makkreel's *Imagination and Interpretation in Kant* (1990), which I believe has
profound implications for the development of the normative human

and social sciences. Makkreel develops a model of orientation in judg‐
ment that links reflective judgment to Kant's notion of the *sensus communis* and thereby to an interpretative community. I will attempt
to show how such a model, originally rooted in Kant's judgments con‐
cerning political phenomena, can be extended to issues of moral de‐
velopment through emerging cosmopolitan public consciousness.
Perhaps, then, this is really three books.

Introduction:
Brief History of the Criticism
of Moral Progress in History

Many have argued that Kant's writings on history are incompatible with his ethical theory and therefore have no systematic value for his philosophy. This perspective has a long lineage going back to Emil von Fackenheim's article "Kant's Concept of History," in which he argues that a rational (moral) man must be free and responsible without qualification.[1] If this is so, historical development either qualifies moral freedom or morality—to the extent that it is possible—does not develop historically. Following the first line of reasoning, some have inferred that Kant's views on the moral development of the species violate the postulate of the moral equality of all men.[2]

Fackenheim concludes that Kant's attempts to introduce moral causality into the world of experience are not successful. He argues that because cultural and other institutional forms of outer freedom can arise without the development of a good will, they cannot provide the necessary mediating links between the realm of appearance and the realm of morality. Since, according to Fackenheim, morality is equivalent to the subjective character of a good will, moral goodness is an attribute only of individuals, not of institutions or groups. Although nature, by providing man with the capacity for choice, can prepare the ground of outer freedom, these forms of freedom fail to express moral value insofar as the development of outer freedom, discipline, and culture are merely self-serving. To the extent that all historical accomplishment is viewed as merely the product of self-interest, there exists no systematic ground uniting historical development and morality. Kant's theory of radical evil further muddies the waters, since the ascription of this propensity to the entire species appears to give little room for hope that genuine moral progress is possible in historical terms. Fackenheim concludes that Kant's construction of a history of freedom is of dubious value from both a speculative and a moral point of view.

William Galston in his book-length study of the idea of history in Kant's philosophy, *Kant and the Problem of History,* echoes these themes.[3] Although he is sensitive to the problem of moral skepticism, which the idea of a progressive history is intended to overcome, Galston too concludes that the Kantian project of reconciliation fails. It does so on two grounds. According to Galston, Kant fails to clarify the source of moral progress per se. Like Fackenheim, Galston argues that the very principles of Kantian ethics, derived from the concept of a morally good will, make it neither necessary nor possible to ascribe central significance to the realm of historical actions and events. Moral progress can only be an individual affair. The realm of human history, then, does not qualify as an arena of moral progress. In addition, Galston assumes that history consists of a series of immoral acts; because they cannot be viewed as the product of a good will, they cannot be ascribed to a free will. Evil from this perspective is caused by passions that are themselves strictly subject to mechanical determination. This makes history a force external to the will and removes the burden of moral accountability from the historical realm. The "good" will cannot be known to be efficacious and the "bad" will is not a free or accountable will. The identification of a free will with a morally good disposition creates a fatal disjunction between morality and history. It would appear that Kant's own notion of "radical evil" as the character of the human species undermines any attempt to theorize about the development of moral freedom and thus moral progress in the historical realm.

While Galston's complaint that Kant fails to mark out a clear and unambiguous path from institutional to moral progress is justified, Kant clearly articulates in several of his essays on history a belief that moral progress in history is possible. The difficulty in picking out the trajectory of moral progress in Kant's works stems from the tendency to identify the good will, insofar as it is the source of moral progress in history, with the moral dispositions of individuals. Since the moral dispositions of individuals are not available to inspection, speculations concerning moral progress on this dimension have no empirical manifestation, hence no historical significance. However, in the essay specifically devoted to the question of the moral progress of humanity, "An Old Question Raised Again," Kant not only defended the French Revolution as a sign of moral progress but attributed this advance to the "moral character of humanity" as demonstrated by the public response of disinterested sympathy.[4] Since historical progress is an attribute of the species, the source of this progress must be in some moral attribute of humanity that, for judgments of moral development, is the functional equivalent of the good will. In this essay, Kant identifies the human predisposition to morality as a historically operative cause. The claim that the species has moral attributes in the form of predispositions is developed in Kant's *Religion* and will be explicated further in chapter 2. The identification of the predisposition to morality as a "moral cause" does not provide a clear line of prediction from one event to another. It does, however, provide the basis for rational hope that further efforts of a similar kind will occur and thus provides a kind of base line for individual duty. This predisposition allows Kant "to attribute to man an inherent and unalterably good, albeit, limited will."[5] This " limited" yet good will gets Kant beyond the prediction problem by providing mankind with a capacity to be the cause of its own improvement, a cause that cannot be eradicated or diminished in its effectiveness. Thus the generic judgment that moral progress in history is possible is not dependent upon specific achievements. Given the timeless character of this moral cause, all that is required for progress to ensue is for the appropriate circumstances to occur, which barring natural catastrophe, have a significant probability in the life of the species. To the extent that individuals can identify circumstances appropriate for the promotion of moral goals, individual duty can be meaningfully shaped and action can be coordinated to attain historical ends. This type of knowing *what is appropriate* depends upon a relationship between purposiveness and progress that it is the function of reflective judgment to disclose. The cognitive status of reflective judgment and the role of reflective judgment in Kant's philosophy of history will be developed in later chapters.

For the skeptic, these considerations shift the problem of moral progress to Kant's right to treat mankind as a moral species. I will attempt to demonstrate in chapter 2 that the claim that mankind is a moral species is implicit in the foundations of Kantian ethics and that individual moral perfection cannot ultimately be disconnected from the possibilities inherent in the concept of social and historical progress. In other words, for all of its complexity and tensions, Kant's ethics cannot be meaningfully separated from his philosophy of history.

Galston's second point, concerning the nature of historical evil, is in need of revision. Moral evil, *including its historical manifestations*, cannot be viewed as the result of mechanical causes. While commentators recognize that, on the individual level, moral evil is to be ascribed to the "free" will, the collective consequences of individual free acts—historical

evil in the form of social and institutional injustice—is frequently analyzed in terms of the "cunning of nature." In "Idea for a Universal
History" Kant refers to man's "unsocial sociability" as the means that
nature uses to bring about the development of human capacities and
a lawful order.[6] This reference to nature is often taken to represent
Kant's view that evil as a historical force has a natural basis that makes
progressive development possible without moral motivation or intention. Insofar as this interpretation suggests that nature causes either
moral good (through unintended consequences) or evil, it removes
human responsibility for historical events.

This interpretation of nature's use of evil as a progressive force,
while a common theme in the Kantian literature, is recognized to be
in tension with Kant's mature view on the nature of moral progress,
which must include principled action. Yirmiahu Yovel's extended study
Kant and the Philosophy of History increased appreciation for the historical
dimensions of reason itself. Arguing that critical reason has a history,
Yovel claimed that conscious rational principles once developed could
become explanations for human action within Kant's historical system.[7] More recently, Paul Guyer has argued that by the time Kant
wrote "Perpetual Peace" he had revised the claim of "Idea for a Universal History" concerning the causal role of natural mechanisms in making peace possible. What appears in the later essay, according to Guyer,
is "the more restricted proposition that nature is at least compatible
with the achievement of global justice because it affords us mechanisms which can be exploited by moral politicians with a commitment to the end of justice."[8]

As we learn from Kant's later exposition of the nature of evil in the
Religion, moral evil cannot be derived from nature per se but only
from the free exercise of certain predispositions. The Kantian conception of moral evil as outlined in the *Religion* defines moral evil as a
"propensity," an acquired characteristic of the faculty of freedom so
fundamental that it is coeval with the social and cultural condition of
man.[9] At no point in time, then, is either the individual or the human
species exempt from moral responsibility for the existence of evil. In
"Conjectural Beginning of Human History," published just two years
after "Idea," Kant says of the difference between natural and human
history: "The history of nature therefore begins with good, for it is the
work of God, while the history of freedom begins with wickedness, for
it is the work of man."[10]

Both *Religion* and "Conjectural Beginning" view evil not as the result of a nature external to human volition, but as a characteristic of
the exercise of that volition that has left its mark on human culture
and history.

While each individual is accountable for the influence of this propensity on his or her actions, moral evil cannot be understood in a reductive individualist sense. The impact of moral evil on the social and cultural life of man is of grave concern to the individual both as an impediment to his or her own moral development and as a source of significant moral duties of a social nature. Nonetheless, the fact that our social life provides evidence of a fundamental moral corruption that supersedes the powers of the isolated individual to remedy does not render the character of social life a mechanically determined artifact. Although it is arguable that Kant's views on the contribution of nature to moral progress may have changed from "Idea for a Universal History" to the writing of "Perpetual Peace," references to nature in the essays on history are generally best understood as reflective interpretations of the social context of human action. In these essays, "Nature's intentions" are expressed in the language of teleological "purposiveness." But teleology for Kant is a subjective principle whose significance is only fully cashed out in a practical context. Such interpretations of what nature may or may not do to advance moral goals may indirectly support ethical analysis by suggesting ways that the natural context can be used to overcome impediments to moral improvement, but they cannot substitute for a direct ethical analysis of culture or history. Kant's philosophy of history and culture is an extension of his practical philosophy, with all its normative implications for the nature of historical reflective judgment.

After attributing the propensity to evil to the character of the species, Kant postulates a victory over the "evil principle" in the form of a social union that it is the duty of the species to attain. Because humanity is a moral species, each person has obligations for the common good and individuals are accountable for the condition of the species. That the achievement of this social union is a "collective" duty does not mean that we cannot identify distributive duties that are contributions to this end. Viewing the highest good as a social goal, Gerald Barnes has argued that the concept of a collective duty can be analyzed distributively with individuals deriving specific duties from their membership in particular ethical communities.[11] Precisely because as individuals we are fettered by the propensity to evil, we are directly obligated to promote those objectives which, through the transformation of our social condition, enhance the moral development of humanity. The implications of Kant's view of the moral attributes and character of the species and its bearing on the duties of individuals have yet to be adequately assimilated into Kant's overall social and historical philosophy. Both the predisposition to morality and the propensity to evil play significant roles in orienting the individual toward collective moral goals. It is the intention of this book to undertake this assimilation.

If the objections of Fackenheim and Galston cannot be adequately addressed, they generate a bit of a scandal.[12] Their claims imply that Kant's views on the moral development of humanity, including the idea of a highest moral good, are groundless. This view that the highest good is at best superfluous to Kantian ethics has had staunch defenders. In his classic commentary on Kant's *Critique of Practical Reason*, Lewis White Beck argued that the highest good created no duties in addition to those already specified by Kant's metaphysics of morals and was therefore irrelevant to individual duty.[13] John Silber, however, defended the practical character of the highest good as a stimulant to moral striving, because it challenged the limits of human freedom.[14] Thomas Auxter in turn criticized just this ideal quality of the highest good. He maintained that the emphasis on intensity of motive rather than intelligible outcomes was damaging to serious moral effort to reshape the world.[15] In his systematic study of moral teleology in Kant, Auxter thoroughly analyzes but rejects the notion of the highest good.[16] According to Auxter, the retributivist implications of some versions of the highest good work against a strong sense of social community. He nonetheless retains a vigorous social-historical ethic by replacing the role of the highest good with the concept of an ectypical world and a robust doctrine of essential ends.

Although contemporary interpreters have taken an increasingly sympathetic approach to the historical significance of Kant's concept of the highest good, none have provided an adequate explanation of how such a goal is related to the moral life of individuals. In "What do the Virtuous Hope For?" Pauline Kleingeld presents a good contemporary summary of the problems associated with the highest good and mounts a vigorous defense of this concept.[17] In particular, she demonstrates how happiness can be understood to be compatible with the nonhedonistic foundations of Kantian ethics. Arguing that the pursuit of virtue transforms our conceptions of happiness, Kleingeld notes how this transformation points in the direction of the "interdependence" of the happiness of oneself and others. The social context of happiness is thus secured, but the social context of virtue remains relatively unarticulated. Kleingeld notes Kant's claim that there is a duty to join an ethical community "which aims at the moral 'improvement' of humankind and at fending off evil" but ultimately fails to see this as a systematic requirement for moral life. She concludes that "Kant's argument for the existence of a duty to promote the highest good seems to depend on the construction of the idea of a moral world, but Kant does not present an argument to show that all humans qua finite rational beings do or should construct such an idea."[18]

The missing part of the argument for the construction of this "moral world" as a necessary "final end" is the personal as well as collective significance of the ethical commonwealth for the overcoming of evil. We might call this Kant's argument from radical evil. Since the highest good is conditioned upon the existence of virtue, it presupposes the overcoming of evil. Since moral evil cannot be overcome without the realization of the ethical commonwealth, overcoming evil is more than an act of individual renunciation. Moral development requires the simultaneous promotion of ethical forms of community. Virtue therefore goes beyond traditional analyses of duties of beneficence even when these are extended, refined, and defended on nonhedonistic grounds, because moral development extends beyond the individual paradigm. That radical evil affects the entire species binds the destiny of each to all both as a matter of global interdependence and as a matter of historical legacy. Historical institutions therefore must develop within the context of universal ethical communities. This means that genuine solutions to the problem of evil will require international institutions dedicated to intergenerational economic justice and ecologically sustainable development. These issues will be specifically addressed in the concluding chapter.

To make the highest good a systematic requirement of moral life one must argue for an intrinsic connection between the highest good and individual duty. For this argument to succeed it is necessary to explain how one can contribute to a task that is simultaneously of personal value and of collective significance, such that the overcoming of evil for the individual is a contribution to moral progress for the species. This requires the identification of a goal that has these characteristics on both the personal and collective level and a form of practical cognition that can apprehend the nature of a contribution toward this goal. Although there is a long tradition of connecting Kant's idea of the highest good with his philosophy of history, it has not been clearly articulated how it is that individuals have a personal stake in the promotion of this ideal. Something is needed that bypasses the retributive elements of the highest good while capturing the directly personal level that a moral goal operates upon. This historical "vehicle" is the ethical commonwealth, which provides a personal stake in the highest good because it is designed as both a social goal and the means for the overcoming of evil for the individual. The duty to enter into ethical community upon the terms of the ethical commonwealth is a special type of personal duty that springs directly out of the confrontation with evil, specifically out of our awareness that we cannot seek self-perfection without simultaneously seeking the conditions of the perfection of others. Virtue is a collective task because evil is a pervasive feature of human social interaction and the institutions that develop from these interactions. Since Kantian ethics is generally thought to be primarily an ethics of individual achievement, there is much in what I have said to be defended. My particular interpretation of moral evil, which emphasizes the social context of evil, will be defended in chapter 3. But beyond the textual analysis drawn primarily from the *Religion*, which provides significant support, my interpretation of moral evil draws its strength from the way that it makes sense of Kant's views on moral progress in history. Progress in history can be moral only insofar as the principal moral task for the individual is itself also a collective task—that is, if there exists a moral task that operates simultaneously on the personal and social level. This can only be the collective overcoming of evil in the formation of an ethical commonwealth. This formulation of the problem of evil makes Kantian moral philosophy, a social philosophy at its foundations and provides a more coherent framework for his philosophy of history.

In my previous work on Kant's concept of the highest good, I argued that many of the objections to the highest good assume that virtue, even where the object is some social good, is primarily an individual task. I maintained that to fully appreciate the significance of the highest good in moral life requires creating a model of virtue as a collective achievement, in terms of which individuals view themselves as part of a larger community, an ethical commonwealth.[19] By bringing the highest good out of the realm of an unattainable ideal and into connection with particular ethical communities, the role of this concept as a regulative principle of historical action can be better appreciated.

While my interpretation of moral progress in Kant's philosophy of history will continue to make use of the idea of a highest good, I will draw primarily upon the concept of the highest moral good as defined in the *Religion*, where the "good" of this concept is most clearly a social good. The social core of this concept provides the basis for its historical content. In book 3 of the *Religion*, the highest moral good is defined as a social good, a unification of dispositions into a community under principles of virtue.[20] With respect to this social good, references to a physical happiness exactly proportioned to virtue (with the retributivist connotations rejected by Auxter) are absent. If, in this context, virtue is its own reward, it is not merely the inner satisfaction of individual conscientiousness but also the shared satisfaction of a common good in the form of a united community. In this context, the individual's search for perfection is directly connected to the achievement of social goals. What one contributes to this social good is then what one contributes to one's perfection. Clearly this interpretation of the highest good as the goal and consequence of an ethical community entails a radical transformation in our conceptions of happiness that makes considerably more intelligible Kant's claim that in a moral world virtuous individuals will be the cause of happiness.

This community of virtue, or ethical commonwealth, is to be approximated through historical ethical communities, each dedicated to the social good. So understood, moral progress is marked through social progress, and individual virtue will entail duties to contribute to this historical development. The tension between Kant's philosophy of history and ethics, between the moral development of the species and that of individuals, can ultimately only be overcome by demonstrating how these historical ideals are related to the duties of individuals and how specific forms of their realization can be apprehended.

We can then show that Kant was not really of two minds on the topic of moral development, shifting unconsciously from the model of individual moral development to that of the species. While some of Kant's references to moral development may be appropriate only to individuals, we must also assume that individual moral development, insofar as it includes obligations to a social good, will entail a moral development of the species. In "An Old Question Raised Again," we find Kant expressing what must seem to be a strange conviction, given the once traditional view of the unbridgeable rift between historical development and moral freedom, between the individual and the species. As noted earlier, in this essay Kant maintains that it can be demonstrated that the human species in fact progresses and displays a moral character.[21] Since the species begins its development from a condition of moral evil, we must ask what this reference to "progress" implies about the character of the species. Can the "character" of the species be both good and evil? Kant was notoriously "rigorist" concerning the disposition or "intelligible" character of individuals. The individual disposition must be either good or evil. But then the individual disposition never "appears" in time. If the propensity to evil is responsible for the merely "empirical" character of the species, what then is the source of the moral "progress" of the species and how do we come to ascertain that such a source is active? By means of a theory of historical "signs" Kant maintains that there is some marker whereby we can discern the presence of this source—that is, the "moral predisposition" of the species. In chapter 1 I will analyze the nature of the cognitive act underlying Kant's theory of historical signs through which we apprehend the moral progress of the species, and I will indicate how knowledge about the development of the species impacts the duties of individuals.

The concept of radical evil profoundly affects the entire relationship between Kant's philosophy of history and ethics. For if we must assume that individuals begin their exercise of freedom in a shared condition of moral evil, then the concept of radical evil raises serious doubt concerning the standard view of individual moral development as the centerpiece of Kantian ethics. At a minimum, the condition of the species would be a significant factor in the development of the moral life of the individual.[22] Although the propensity to evil, as understood in the *Religion*, is a subjectively necessary feature of human freedom, the good news is that evil is not a defining attribute of the concept of man and so does not limit human potential.[23] The predispositions that are "elements in the fixed character and destiny of man" are not only "good in a negative fashion . . . they are also predispositions toward the good."[24] Moral evil, Kant maintains, can be eliminated. In fact, it is a duty of the species, collectively, and of every individual, distributively, to work toward its eradication. Individuals then have a moral interest in the condition of the species, which provides the social context for the specification of duty.

It is the purpose of this book to demonstrate that Kantian ethics is not complete without a philosophy of history that provides a context rooted in the human social condition for individual judgment and moral action. While Kant's problems and insights inspire this work, I do not maintain that Kant has provided a complete and systematic rendition of the perspective on moral development that I will argue for. This book is a reconstruction based on Kant's writings, and I attempt to bring as much system and coherence to these works as they can bear. My conclusions will at times go beyond anything that Kant has actually stated. In my final chapter, I will extend this model of moral development to the issues facing us at the close of the twentieth century.

Chapter 1 will investigate the cognitive status of the principles underlying Kant's philosophy of history. Chapter 2 will consider how Kant's concept of moral autonomy was extended to include the highest good as a social and historical object. Chapter 3 will demonstrate how Kant's *Religion* provides the basis for a social perspective on the problem of evil and a historical goal for its overcoming. Chapter 4 will analyze Kant's view on the origins of culture and how cultural differentiation shapes humanity's moral goals. Chapter 5 will consider how political evolution is related to the idea of moral progress. Chapter 6 will connect the goals of international law and human rights to the emergence of a cosmopolitan public. The conclusion will consider how the achievement of specific historical goals determines the scope and nature of the moral duties of individuals in our contemporary context.

1

Purposiveness and Cognition

Recent scholarship has shown a renewed interest in Kant's philosophy of history, concepts of teleology, and the role of imagination and judgment in the Critical System. John Zammito's *The Genesis of Kant's Critique of Judgment* and Rudolf Makkreel's *Imagination and Interpretation in Kant* are good examples of the current emphasis on the purposive character of cognitive structures.[1] The spontaneous conformity to law of the imagination in aesthetic judgment, according to Zammito, illustrates the intrinsic organization, ends, and purposes of the human mind. Beauty is purposive in contributing to our awareness of moral feeling and our acceptance of moral principles, precisely because the feelings evoked in both are "cognate," that is, derived from the same original powers of the mind.[2] The transcendental potential of feeling to bear the mark of a relation to reason is fundamental to our awareness of empirical freedom and our status as practical–purposive agents.[3]

Makkreel foregrounds the feeling of life as providing the general framework for understanding the reflective powers of the imagination. Life, Makkreel explains, is expanded in Kant's *Critique of Judgment* beyond its biological meanings to include and primarily signify the spontaneity of the mind. The feeling of life is the fount of reflection and orientation that allows judgment to evaluate the significance of things in relation to self and world.[4]

In addition to its aesthetic employment, both authors develop the role of judgment in estimating the moral significance of cultural and historical products. The thesis that our cognitive structures and our moral interests are purposive in nature provides greater systematic

13

coherence to Kant's works. Zammito maintains that the final "ethical turn" in Kant's thinking about the nature of judgment was necessitated by his concern for the ultimate "unity of reason." In particular, the common purposive structure of cognitive acts of estimation and evaluation opens up and supports important investigations into the normative status of the social and historical dimensions of Kant's philosophy that are crucial to any applications of Kantian ethical theory to social and political conditions on a global and universal level.

Traditional perspectives neglecting the philosophy of history had contributed to a sharp separation of Kant's ethical theory from his social–historical theorizing. The moral goals of historical development, such as perpetual peace, are from this perspective objects of "hope." They do not entail specific duties or a theory of social action.[5]

Because ethical principles result from a distinctive function of reason, "practical reason," different in character from the cognitive acts whereby in general we apprehend the nature of the physical world, the cognitive processes that determine duty seem to have little to do with the cognitive processes that present the social and historical context for action. This presumed disjunction of cognitive acts that apprehend the nature of the historical cultural world from the cognitive acts that determine moral value has resulted in a theoretical separation of (social) facts from values and a detachment of both from any general and inclusive normative system. Such a detachment encourages the study of human action from the "outside" as a merely physical phenomena and thereby generates a social scientific behaviorism bereft of both purposiveness and values. Moral value then is not to be found reflected in the phenomenal world but is relegated to its own realm.

Values abstracted from their social context are difficult then to reapply in a world of cultural diversity and political conflict. With the ejection of moral values from the realm of social theorizing and with no benchmarks for moral improvement in human affairs, cultural relativism with its "tolerance" principle is recommended as the best or negative substitute for a genuine or positive theory of human rights. But tolerance, because it does not entail an active engagement with the good of others, can easily degenerate into indifference and inaction.

Respect for human rights would seem to entail some principle for contextualizing rights that recognizes the value of culture in shaping human identity, while allowing for the institutional mediation of conflicts arising from diversity. To create the institutional forms that can promote human rights we need a theory of historical development that can connect cultural pluralism and political change with the realm of moral values. If the principles by which we evaluate social and cultural institutions are not in some sense derivative from our moral ideals, then though we may project moral goals and ends as "ideal" targets of human action, we will have no means to chart the course that would realize these ideals. We will have in effect no way to "orient" our action toward the open horizon of the moral ideal.

Kant's moral ideals cannot be separated from his perspective on historical development. Because these ideals characterize the condition of the species as a whole, they can only be approximated in and through historical activity. But even an "approximation" requires that the duties of particular individuals are connected in some discernible way to specific historical goals. These specific historical goals must be "known" to count as approximations of these ideals. This presupposes that there is a form of historical knowledge that is capable of recognizing the contribution of specific institutions toward moral goals, a form of knowledge that apprehends the "moral purposiveness" of particular phenomena. How then do we apprehend the purposive character of historical activity? There must then be a cognitive framework appropriate to the special status of human action as both an empirical phenomena and a manifestation of transcendental freedom.

The development of human freedom is the theme of Kant's philosophy of history. Human action is an object of experience. It occurs within the natural world and therefore must occur in conformity with natural laws. In "Idea for a Universal History," Kant tells us that "Whatever concept one may hold, from a metaphysical point of view, concerning the freedom of the will, certainly its appearances, which are human actions, like every other natural event are determined by universal laws."[6] It is equally fundamental to Kant's critical philosophy that human actions are "effects of freedom." Human actions are not mechanically determined, as that form of causality excludes the spontaneity characteristic of freedom. For the casual observer, the effect of free will on human action makes individual choices appear random and chaotic. But what is random and chaotic is not, at least for our understanding, "determined by universal laws."

Kant's solution to the problem of the lawfulness of human freedom is to adopt the standpoint of the "human race as a whole," to attend to "the play of freedom of the human will in the large" and to the "progressive though slow evolution of its original endowment."[7] From this perspective Kant claims that we will discover a regular movement in the aggregate. Human actions will then appear lawful. But what form of lawfulness is this? What sort of "object of experience" is the human race as a whole? In assessing the "appearances of freedom," Kant has in fact abandoned a mechanistic framework and adopted a teleological perspective on human action connecting freedom with

the development of an "original endowment." This "original endowment" entails the development of practical freedom and ultimately the
projection of moral goals that define humanity as a moral species. The
upshot of this is that some phenomena are to be "assessed" or understood in nonmechanistic, teleological, and evaluative terms. Human
history, insofar as this refers to our interpretation of collective human
activity, will not be a part of natural science in a narrow sense. Human
history will be both an empirical and a normative discipline.

Kant's notion of nature, as we know from the *Critique of Judgment*, is
not restricted to that of "events" constituted by mechanistic principles.
Nature refers generally to the lawfulness of experience as such. Mechanical lawfulness is not the only kind of lawfulness that we encounter in the natural world. Although the lawfulness of experience is first
made possible by the categories of the understanding, these categories
do not sufficiently determine the content of particular empirical regularities which may display such a degree of diversity as to make the
organization of experience into a system impossible. The categories
allow us to anticipate the causal character of experience but do not tell
us what particular connections we will find. That empirical regularities can be organized into higher-order laws is, from the point of view
of our finite understanding, a contingent occurrence. That we are con-
tinually successful in discovering such "laws" evokes our wonder. Although these higher-order laws serve the understanding, they are not
the work of the understanding. They do not have a mechanistic character. Not all lawfulness is mechanistic.

The organization of empirical regularities into a system of empirical laws is the work of judgment. Judgment apprehends and subsumes
the particular under a universal rule. As reason is the source of universals, and sensibility the source of particulars, judgment is the ground
of the cognitive harmony between them. According to Kant, judgment
operates in terms of its own principle, the principle of subjective purposiveness. This harmony of our cognitive powers is subjectively necessary in the sense that without it, the organization of experience would
not proceed. Experience constrains or shapes the work of judgment,
but does not provide its principle of operation. Neither sensibility nor
reason can prescribe the principle of the operation of judgment.

In his introduction to the *Critique of Judgment* Kant explains the nature of this principle:

> The judgment has therefore also in itself a principle a priori of
> the possibility of nature, but only in a subjective aspect by
> which it prescribes not to nature (autonomy) but to itself
> (heautonomy) a law for its reflection upon nature. This we

might call the law of the specification of nature in respect of its empirical laws.[8]

Judgment in this sense is "free" and must orient itself to the variety of existing particulars. Makkreel argues that this "orientational function" of judgment is fundamental to Kant's entire transcendental program, because it provides a nonfoundational source of reflection upon the relationship between subject and world. Reflective judgment, he maintains, provides the context from which scientific knowledge can arise from "our pre understanding of the life world as modes of transcendental orientation."[9]

Judgment then is a cognitive ground for certain purposive principles that do not constitute nature but structure our apprehension and guide our investigative practices. Due to the multidimensional function of judgment in the organization and operation of experience, purposiveness is a pervasive feature of human consciousness.

Science as an organized investigation of nature depends upon both the mechanistic categories of the understanding (to provide for the possibility of experience as such) and the purposive principles of judgment (to provide the actual organization of experience as a system). The harmony that judgment produces and pursues is, moreover, a dynamic harmony. For if reason were not in a sense actively demanding a type of unity not immediately given, the work of judgment as a "felt" harmony between the faculties would go unnoticed. Purposiveness is judgment's quiet response to reason's need for organization.

But the unique character of judgment comes to the foreground in several areas of human experience. Judgment is busy in the activity of science, provides pleasure in the experience of beautiful objects, and evokes wonder in the estimation of organic beings. The first of these three areas derives from the active or purposive character of reason itself, revealing reason's constructive role in regulating experience.

> Reason has, therefore, as its sole object, the understanding and its effective application. Just as the understanding unifies the manifold in the object by means of concepts, so reason unifies the manifold of concepts by means of ideas, positing a certain collective unity as the goal of the activities of the understanding, which otherwise are concerned solely with distributive unity.[10]

But the latter two areas appear to call for a different mode of explanation. Here unity is not so much demanded as encountered. The encounter with beauty and with organic beings suggests that *something in nature* accords with the purposiveness of human consciousness. While Kant did not infer from this that beauty has an independent existence in the object or that mechanistic principles could not be applied to investigate living things, he did maintain that our conscious apprehension of some phenomena is mediated by a principle of purposiveness. Some phenomena present themselves to consciousness as something more than mechanisms. As Irmagard Scherer has recently argued, such phenomena have a cognitive significance rooted in the independent yet pervasive power of judgment as an attribute of consciousness. She maintains:

> [P]urposiveness is a fixed and real condition in human consciousness, regulating the manifold of experience. . . . The governing principle of purposiveness resides in the judgment which is an independent part of consciousness in contact with both the sensible and the supersensible through its own a priority.[11]

Some objects, then, are purposive *in their particular phenomenal character.* Nature is purposive in its systematic character and also, as an organic realm, in its particular phenomenal products. Organisms can only be apprehended on the assumption that they are individual systems whose parts reciprocally determine one another. Kant explains: "For a body then which is judged in itself and its internal possibility as a natural purpose, it is requisite that its parts mutually depend upon one another both as to their form and their combination and so produce a whole by their own causality, while conversely the concept of the whole may be regarded as its cause according to a principle."[12]

Since purpose is for our cognition a product of reason and not of the understanding, the concept of a natural purpose cannot be derived "objectively" from the a priori concept of nature in general. The internal purposiveness of an organism is unlike both the mechanical and intentional concepts of causality, and since these are, according to Kant, the only types of causality available to us, the concept of a natural purpose is not strictly speaking a causal concept at all. Since purposiveness is not a category of the understanding, it is not a sufficient explanation for the existence of the phenomena. It is rather a ground of cognition. Kant continues:

> Only in this way can the idea of the whole conversely (reciprocally) determine the form and combination of all the parts, not indeed as cause . . . for then it would be an artificial product . . . but as the ground of cognition, for him who is judging

it, of the systematic unity and combination of all the manifold contained in the given manifold.[13]

Although a system of relative or external purposiveness can be constructed to answer hypothetical questions concerning the existence of specific types of organisms (and this assumes the validity of intrinsic purposiveness) even when pursued to the point of nature as a whole, it will not constitute an explanation of organic existence as such. Once external purposiveness is introduced systematically, the chain of purposes can only terminate in a being whose existence[14] is not a relative purpose, but rather an end in itself. The only possible candidate for this designation is man, the very being whose consciousness has introduced purposiveness into experience to begin with.

What then does it mean to be an end in itself? Is purposiveness a mere phenomenon of consciousness, a reflecting mirror of nature whose grounds are forever hidden from view? Perhaps, but Kant believes that the answer to this question can be approached definitively from another point of view; the point of view of moral experience. Human beings are purposeful beings. They set purposes and use nature for their own ends. This gives to human action a form of relative independence from nature. If all human purposes were arbitrary or merely contingent upon a natural cause, humanity would not deserve to be called an end in itself. If, however, human purposes are themselves part of a system of unconditioned value determined by an unconditioned law, humanity can rightly be considered an end in itself. In the *Groundwork of the Metaphysics of Morals*, Kant maintains that such an unconditioned law, which sets humanity apart from nature, can be derived from the character of moral experience. This unconditioned law, the moral law, determines the proper purposes of humanity and makes human freedom more than a natural phenomenon.

The moral law provides both an ontological and a cognitive warrant for the ascription of freedom to the human will. The capacity to give the law to oneself, autonomy, is a condition of the possibility of this unconditioned law. Though the ontological grounds of freedom in pure practical reason, *Wille*, are noumenal, in its practical manifestation as *Willkur* the human will for Kant remains phenomenal. Since man is both a natural purpose (an organic being) and an end of pure practical reason (a moral being) he combines in his own peculiar essence nature and reason. This double nature is entailed in Kant's reference to man in the *Critique of Judgment* as nature's ultimate purpose. This final designation implies more than that man is a natural product. In calling man nature's "ultimate" purpose, Kant implies that in man nature is conjoined with morality, because only on this assumption can there be an overall or "ultimate" purpose in a natural realm. Kant explains: "The commonest judgment of healthy reason completely accords with this, that it is only as a moral being that man can be a final purpose of creation."[15]

If it is to include the human dimension, nature's systematic purposiveness must be apprehended from a moral point of view. Of course, nature separated from humanity could never appear as a system at all.

The cognitive significance of the principle of natural purposiveness is subjective, derived by analogy from our experience of moral self–determination. But this does not make it arbitrary. Were natural purposiveness a constitutive or objective principle man's phenomenal freedom would be but an extension of nature's real or actual purpose. This would itself be a "metaphysical" postulate with devastating implications for human moral accountability. This limitation of natural purposiveness to a merely cognitive role has, then, a positive function. It places the ground of freedom beyond nature, while requiring that nature in its immediate (organic) relation to man be conceived in nonmechanistic terms. Since human purposeful action is *causal through concepts* (this is how practical reason is defined), how we think of nature is an important attribute of how we conceive of ourselves as agents and construct the context for action. In purposeful action we do not see ourselves as "cogs in a machine." Purposiveness is the cognitive precondition that enables us to set ends. We share a purposiveness with nature that allows us to discover patterns and laws that support our activity. Nature does not contradict but invites this formulation of a purposive ground for human action. We are invited to discover in the purposive patterns of our experience the appropriate materials for our own objectively determined practical ends.

Purposiveness as a transcendental principle lies at the root of all of our cognitive faculties. It is the mediating link between man and nature from both a theoretical and practical perspective. Purposiveness is the character of man's being in the world, providing for the possibility of the formulation of moral intentions that can be set within a natural context.

The purposive character of nature when conceived as a system raises the question of the ultimate purpose of existence. Such a question, I have noted, points to man's role as the only being that can serve as an actual ultimate purpose. But man can only serve in this capacity as a moral species acting collectively to realize moral goals. So whether or not an actual ultimate purpose exists does not depend upon any metaphysics of nature per se but on the character of human history as a progressive realization of moral purposes. Much then depends upon the status attributed to the historical judgment of moral progress. What is the nature of such a judgment?

In his study of the role of imagination and interpretation in Kant's *Critique of Judgment*, Rudolf Makkreel has disclosed an important function of reflective judgment in producing an "authentic interpretation of history." Claiming that it is only by adding the practical perspective that human purposiveness can be fully defined in relation to the purposiveness of nature, Makkreel argues that Kant's claim that man is the ultimate purpose of nature "involves the intersection of a reflective teleological judgment about man as a natural purpose with a determinate judgment of practical reason about man as a final purpose."[16]

Teleological ideas, according to Makkreel, are necessary to provide descriptions of empirical historical processes in relation to human ends and to guide reflection on what we as a community hold to be true about man's actual purposes. Reflective judgment orients historical interpretation by selecting particulars that serve the ends set by determinative practical judgments. Such reflective judgments can then be offered to the community as articulations of moral ideals that are pro gressively realized by human activity. "It is only by prescribing a principle of purposiveness to ourselves that we can reflect on the telos of nature and history."[17] This process of the authentication of historical interpretation seems to me to involve a twofold work of reflective judgment. At the level of the apprehension of particular events, judgment must be able to discern a moral purposiveness in certain phenomena that would allow these to be offered to the judging community as "signs" of moral progress.[18] In addition, such events would have to enter into an open public discourse through which the moral sense of the community can be articulated.

Human action is the subject matter of history. We have argued that human action must be evaluated in a morally purposive context. In order to estimate the moral value of human deeds, the faculty of judgment must be able to apprehend a form of external moral purposiveness in the phenomena of human action. This external moral purposiveness does not refer to the dispositions of individual agents. It is not an estimation of subjective moral merit; rather, it is an estimation of the fit between what human beings collectively create, their cultural and political productions, and moral goals. In identifying this "fit," judgment is operating in its *reflective* capacity, disclosing a necessary but subjective harmony between the form of experience manifest in these productions and a moral ideal.[19] Certain phenomena are apprehended through reflective judgment as historical "signs" of (collective) moral goals, just as reflective judgment apprehends certain phenomena as embodying beauty. Both types of judgment are normative in their structure, providing an a priori ground for intersubjective agreement on the character of human experience.[20] A particular historical interpretation is authenticated in Makkreel's sense when it provides the basis for intersubjective consensus that an event has contributed to the moral interests of humanity. This does not reduce historical judgment to aesthetic appreciation, although it does provide some insight into the various senses in which normative judgments are deeply embedded in human consciousness and community.

The moral goals that the reflective historical judgment is concerned to disclose are those that mankind can only attain collectively, that is, republicanism, justice, international law, human rights, peace, and so forth. These types of goals can only be promoted by individuals, they cannot be attained by individual action alone. These moral–historical goals are foreshadowed in the *Critique of Practical Reason* by Kant's conception of the highest good: the exact proportion of happiness to virtue, which, he maintains, is the necessary object of the moral law. By bringing man's natural aspiration to happiness within the purview of the moral law, Kant underscores the systematic character of pure practical reason.[21] In this way the moral law is intended to be efficacious in the world, providing for the ultimate unity of nature and freedom.

But man's nature as a finite and dependent creature makes the legitimate pursuit of happiness a social activity, an issue of social justice. Auxter has argued (in his exposition of Kant's concept of the highest good as an ectypal nature) for an ethic of inclusive ends, a maximal integration of all the specific purposes of rational agents into wholes. Such an integration would require a progressive realization and harmonization of natural capacities, necessitating cooperation and collaboration among moral agents for their development.[22] An ethics of inclusive ends expresses Kant's ideal of an "ethical community." Moreover, such a community would require a cosmopolitan form to address issues of cultural diversity and the social–political conflicts that result. As Auxter has argued in his conception of "teleological convergence":

> If the realm of ends is really the "complete determination" of the moral maxim if it really is the ideal of conduct . . .it must include (or have the potential for recognizing) some notion of cultural achievement. . . . On another level it will mean developing an empathetic understanding of the cultures and creations of people at other times and places so that we can appreciate the full range of our humanity and communicate it freely.[23]

An ethics of inclusive ends also cannot fail to address the nature and role of moral evil as an impediment to the realization of this moral goal. In particular we need to know what frustrates human collaboration and how cultural conflicts can be justly adjudicated.

In developing the notion of the highest good as a social goal in the *Religion*, Kant specifically noted that man's nature as a finite rational being entails an extension of the moral law that includes a final end as the goal of all of our moral actions.[24] By situating particular actions in a context of final ends, purposiveness is identified a necessary feature of intentional action, and the highest good is placed in a historical context. However, the *Religion* also deepens the problematic of the achievement of this social goal by tackling the concept of moral evil. For it is not nature per se that hinders our promotion of the highest good. It is human nature, in the form of the propensity to evil, that fragments our best efforts at collaboration. It is this "propensity," universally ascribed to humanity, which must be transformed by concerted moral action.

Nature's purposiveness provides mankind with the capacity to set ends. Nature may be imaginatively projected as prodding us toward our goals, and even turning some of the consequences of our evil intentions to the good. But the complete character of the social good, defined as a community united by principles of virtue, can never be realized by merely natural means. Failure to realize the complete social good can only be the consequence of the failure of freedom to actualize its moral potential. The nature of moral evil is an issue that has received relatively little attention by commentators but that must be addressed if the full complexity of Kant's social–historical philosophy is to be grasped.[25]

The following chapter will focus on the social context of moral evil and the cultural dimensions of the concept of happiness. An inclusive ethic in its most comprehensive sense can only be articulated in terms of a historical development that provides a context for the progressive realization of this complex social–cultural end.

2

From Autonomy to
Radical Evil

The appearance of Kant's *Religion within the Limits of Reason Alone* created a stir among some of Kant's admirers. Fackenheim reports that Schiller regarded the essay as "scandalous" and that, in a letter to Herder, Goethe suggested that Kant had devised the concept of radical evil in order to bring even orthodox Christians into the camp of the Critical Philosophy.[1] The thesis of an evil "innate to the species" appeared to Goethe as a betrayal of the absolute freedom he believed to have been invested in the individual in Kant's *Groundwork of the Metaphysics of Morals*. Although subsequent generations of commentators have introduced more refinement into their critiques, the underlying sentiments and suspicions have remained basically the same. How could the author of the Copernican Revolution in philosophy, who had proclaimed the autonomy of reason, have penned a work in which the entire species is regarded as hobbled? Was this not a denigration of the ideals and spirit of the Enlightenment for which Kant had been regarded as a principal spokesman?

The political program of the Enlightenment was indeed optimistic. In this intellectual climate, the *Groundwork* was read as a glorification of individual reason as a source of freedom. Evil was regarded as a temporary condition that would give way to rational critique. Social-political progress was expected to be an automatic consequence of the critique of tradition and reform of social institutions. This emphasis on individual liberty in turn became a source of the romantic celebration of creative independence. But, paradoxically, the ensuing deep contrast between private subjectivity and an indifferent world that frequently impedes and frustrates our purposes, instead of progressively liberating the human spirit, appears to have set the stage for the modern "alienated" man.

It is my view that far from threatening the promise of autonomy implicit in Kant's view of reason, the concept of radical evil offers a systematic means for evaluating the sources of our historical failures to realize human freedom. Kant's relationship to the Enlightenment is, then, quite complex. Clearly the critique of tradition and of sociopolitical institutions is an important first step on the path to enlightenment. But in articulating the challenge to "use one's own reason,"[2] Kant's analysis of the conditions of enlightenment points beyond the individual and identifies the need for the development of an enlightened public. If evil is rooted in the sociocultural aspects of the human condition, it goes deeper than external institutions. External institutions are the result of sociocultural processes that must become the subject of moral improvement. By reconceptualizing the overcoming of evil as a social process, it is possible to build a bridge between Kant's ethics and his philosophy of history. The conception of virtue as a private struggle within a hopelessly corrupt will, which threatens the individual with a life of futility, must be recast as a social struggle guided by an ennobling vision of a common goal and destiny.

Although the Groundwork does not contain a full-blown analysis of the nature of moral evil, there are already hints that evil must stem from an internal source of resistance. When analyzing the historic importance of his own attempt to uncover the fundamental principle of ethics, Kant refers to a "natural dialectic" of practical reason that tends to obscure the source/meaning of the moral law and ultimately causes us to "quibble" with morality. However, this dialectic should not be interpreted as driven by external nature. As we learn from Kant's later writings, this dialectic is rooted in the desire for happiness (self-love), which as an original constituent of human volition is an expression of "human nature." What the Groundwork does not yet clarify is that happiness is not a simple, passive, sentient state such as "pleasure" but is a complex idea with roots in human freedom. The dynamic quality of happiness is brought forth in the Critique of Practical Reason, in which Kant calls happiness an "ideal" of the imagination. We learn further in the Religion that the idea of happiness not only entails the use of reason but specifically of comparative reason which takes its bearings from social–cultural activities. Although Kant's writings on culture and history began to appear in 1784, it was not until the Religion (1793) that Kant offered a detailed exposition of the "structure" of human volition that allows us to see the internal relationship between human desire, social interaction, and freedom.

The version of the human condition offered in the *Religion*, with its complicated hierarchies of predispositions and propensities, contrasts sharply with the abstract and formal conception of reason believed to be essential to human volition in the *Groundwork*. But the view that the *Religion* implies a revision of Kant's ethical theory implies that the *Groundwork* was intended by Kant as a complete and sufficient moral system. However, Kant's preface to the *Groundwork* provides evidence that Kant did not regard the *Groundwork* in such a light. Indeed, he was at pains to underscore that his purpose, although highly significant from the perspective of an exact clarification of the meaning of morality, is limited to an exposition of its principle. The *Groundwork* is, then, what its title announces: a foundation for a system of moral philosophy that will require further elaboration to validate its "objective reality" in relation to human volition. The *Groundwork* ends with a distinction between two standpoints: the sensible (theoretical) and the intelligible (practical).[3] This distinction is not intended to provide an ontological basis for separate worlds but to establish the perspective from which the new critique will begin.

The burden of demonstrating the "objective reality" of the moral law belongs to the *Critique of Practical Reason*, the materials for which Kant had been preparing but had not yet systematized at the time of the *Groundwork*. When Kant does bring this work to completion, we find that he defines practical reason as a faculty of desire with "interests" vested in the material world. That is to say, Kant defines practical reason *inclusively*, such that the formal components that it has as pure reason are essentially bound to a natural terrain, exciting the will to act. Later, as Kant elaborates the relationship between the formal and material components of the will, further distinctions emerge. In the *Metaphysical Principles of Virtue* Kant will distinguish the pure aspect of will, *Wille*, from the broader faculty of desire, *Willkur*. While the capacity of *Willkur* to be an active cause is dependent upon the rational principle provided by *Wille*, choice is, strictly speaking, an attribute of *Willkur*. It is the attribution of choice to *Willkur* that allows for the will to be phenomenal and provides the locus of moral evil. Kant explains the distinction in the following terms:

> Laws proceed from the will, maxims from choice. In man, choice is free. The will relates to nothing but the law. It cannot be called either free or unfree. . . . Therefore, only choice can be called free.[4]

The passing over from speculation to action marks the characteristic function of reason qua practical. While Kant apparently always regarded the "fact" of the matter—that is, that reason is practical—as evident to sound common sense, a legitimate question can be posed from a reflective, if not skeptical, perspective. How can reason, which is defined by criteria internal to itself, be an operative "cause" or "motive" for a will that must constantly confront conditions that it does not create? If reason is to serve as a foundation for a morality that has "objective reality" for a human will, its causal quality must be demonstrated.

In the *Critique of Practical Reason*, Kant's analysis of the problem of reason qua cause takes a rather dramatic turn. Kant puts forward a claim not found in the *Groundwork*: that reason's legislation for a human will is necessarily connected to the construction of its own object. This object, the highest good, is a schematic representation of the world as it ought to be. I call this turn dramatic because the *Groundwork* appeared to have concluded that our ideas of duty are directly "efficacious." There is no attempt in the *Groundwork* to analyze the purposive character of action or to specify the role of an intended object. What we are left with is the claim that if the will seeks its principle in the character of a material object, it will forfeit its freedom. Therefore freedom is, minimally, freedom from determination by material objects and depends for any positive force on determination by rational principle.[5] This appears to leave no room for the will to be purposive. But Kant clearly believed that all finite rational volition was purposive and that specific action depended upon the projection of ends. To resolve this dilemma of the role of ends in moral volition, Kant later articulated the doctrine of "objective ends," or ends proposed by reason.[6]

The turn toward the question of the "intended object" of moral action in the *Critique of Practical Reason* indicates that reason's struggle to be efficacious is related to the capacity to reenvision the natural terrain of action, the material world, in the form of a practical object. Practical reason, like theoretical reason, is finite and discursive, exercising its powers and capacities in relation to a world that it "shapes" but does not create. It is not until the *Religion* that Kant fully explicates his view that the human will is necessarily "purposive" and that this is a "limitation" shared by every finite rational being. Purposiveness, then, does not signal "heteronomy," but "finitude."[7] Kant explains that while moral principle may tell us how we must act, we require the projection of an end in order to envision the "whither" or the way. We need ends to help us envision results that would be harmonious with duty and thereby to choose a specific course of action. Kant even maintains that this extension of the moral law to include a moral goal is what makes man "an object of experience" and ultimately "gives objective though merely practical reality to the concept of morality as causal in the world."[8] A final end, such as Kant takes the highest good to be, would thus provide a kind of moral orientation for human action by linking the needs of reason to the conditions of material existence. This suggests that the "deduction" of the moral law, the demonstration of its objective validity, must take place in relation to human nature and the structure of human volition. The relationship between the moral law and the highest good informs the moral purposiveness of the human will, resulting in the projected "final end" linking the purposiveness of the human will to human historical action. One might say, then, that the complete "deduction" of the moral law takes place through the construction of a transcendental perspective on history.

Kant carefully prepared the conceptual grounds for his solution of the problem of reason's causality by defining the faculty of desire, practical reason, in the second *Critique* as the power of causing the reality of an object by means of its representation (purposive causality).[9] At the center of both the theoretical and practical perspectives is the human capacity for shaping material according to rational criteria. Representation is a generic term that covers both purely formal and empirical concepts. Although not formal, empirical representations are "rational" in that they can be subordinated and connected in accordance with rational rules (categories). When used as elements of practical reasoning, empirical representations take on a purposive character. The important quality of representations for practical reasoning is their ability to "fit" into purposive maxims that can be universalized. Thus Kant allows that the form of natural law be used as a "type" of intelligible nature when judging the moral quality of particular maxims. This is important not only because "lawfulness" is ingredient in both nature and morality but because practical judgment requires that something be available in actual experience that can serve as the point of application of the law to a specific case. Kant explains that "if common sense did not have something to use in actual experience as an example, it could make no use of the law of pure practical reason in applying it to that experience."[10]

When reconceptualized as elements of maxims, empirical representations can become the "material" for the construction of (practical) objects of volition. When representation precedes action, that which in "effect" is a material consequence is, from a practical perspective, an "end." Practical reason is the capacity to freely set ends and to purposively realize these ends in the world.

For many commentators, the revisionist elements in Kantian ethics begin in the second *Critique* with the positing of an object beyond the purity of intention, which circumscribes autonomy by rigorously isolating the individual from any connection with the world (natural or social). The emphasis on isolation from the world, in the ontological-dualistic interpretation of human volition, with its negative conception of freedom so dear to the emerging political ideals of liberalism, is transformed by the introduction of the "highest good" with its disruptive *Act as if* . If the distinction between the sensible/intelligible were meant to be "ontological," then "purity of intention" might well serve as the appropriate "intelligible" object of volition. But this is not, I believe, a correct interpretation of this distinction as it passes over into the second *Critique*. In the context of the *Critique of Practical Reason*, the "intelligible" signals the practical, which is the *morally purposive representation of the material world*.

Furthermore, the focus on the individual as the centerpiece of Kantian ethics scarcely does justice to the continuous references to "relatedness" that characterize Kant's formulations of morality and autonomy throughout the *Groundwork*. These various formulations, whether referring to the relation of actions or maxims or laws, ultimately point to reason's role in producing "the relation of such beings to one another as ends and means."[11] Relatedness is further underscored by Kant's explicit stipulation that the exercise of autonomy is a legislative activity that carries with it the mark of one's membership in a moral community.[12] Although the language of this section is the "language of the schools" of "metaphysics," the functions attributed to autonomy are unmistakably social and complex. Kantian ethics is social at its core.

In introducing the idea of the highest good as an object of moral volition Kant did more than simply "make room" for happiness as a legitimate pursuit subordinated to the moral law. This notion is also ultimately social in significance. The potential compatibility of morality and happiness is apparent in the *Groundwork*, and Kant had already identified benevolence as a major classification of duty. But the highest good as the "unique object" and "final end" of morality is not any simple combination of virtue and happiness. It defines an entire world in which happiness is proportioned to virtue. Because the moral law is herein considered as setting its own agenda rather than functioning simply as a criteria against which particular maxims are measured, the projected object expresses as morally purposive system. The highest good in such a system becomes a condition in which virtue as the supreme good is the ground from which general happiness follows as a consequence.

Now, we know that such a systematic connection is not found in experience; it is not verified by past history, nor does it exist for the singular virtuous individual. The highest good is not, of course, about an individual's good considered in isolation. It is a condition of being that can only apply to the species as a whole. Happiness, Kant asserts, can never be the ground of virtue. But virtue, under ideal conditions—which, I shall argue, are necessarily ideal *social* conditions—can be the ground of happiness. Nature is powerless to produce the exact proportion between virtue and happiness that the moral law demands. But individual efforts alone are also powerless to produce this proportion. Worthiness is the constraint placed upon the distribution of happiness, which a good will is obligated to promote. There are many problems with this particular formulation of the highest good, not the least of which is that our epistemological limitations render us incapable of making the type of moral assessment of worthiness necessary to be "just distributors."[13] Our obligation to "promote" this type of world cannot mean that individuals should attempt to become the distributing agents.[14] Individual duty is limited to supporting the conditions under which this proportion arises as the result of a morally purposive order. These conditions, which are social in nature, lead us to the duty to contribute to the development of a just world. Were such a world to come into existence it would presumably prove the objective reality of the moral law, for such a world could not arise from nature per se.

I will have more to say later as to how we should interpret the conditions that make virtue possible. But insofar as virtue, the supreme condition of the highest good, is not a simple attribute of isolated individuals conscientiously pursuing the purity of their own intentions, we can assume that some of these conditions pertain to the nature of the social world. And since the social world is also a "cultural world," the connection between the highest good, culture, and history will remain a constant theme of this work.

I have attempted to trace the development of Kant's view of the moral purposiveness of the human will in order to expose the social and historical dimensions that the moral life will necessarily assume. It is not coincidental, then, that the challenge to the moral life that the existence of evil poses is also articulated in social terms. A major thesis of this work is that Kant's theory of evil provides an important interpretative bridge for the historical, cultural, and social dimensions of his moral philosophy. Contemporary moral and social philosophers attempting to "apply Kant" to modern problems have simply assumed a continuity between Kant's individual and social ethics without necessarily recognizing the important interpretative gaps that remain. The virtuous life is not exhausted by extending the reach of the duties of beneficence. How the individual's obligation to pursue moral perfection is connected to the highest good as a social goal must be addressed. This connection is central to any socially oriented Kantian ethics.

Earlier I argued that reason's capacity to be "practical" entails an

"object" and that this is a consequence of the purposive or finite quality of human volition. But why must this object be the "highest good,"
an object seemingly so removed from the individual's powers and
prima facie obligations? In what sense is the individual's prima facie
supreme obligation, to pursue virtue or moral perfection, itself bound
up with a social goal of historic magnitude? The concept of radical evil
as a "species character" can provide an interpretative key.

I shall attempt to demonstrate that the concept of the highest good
is reformulated by Kant in the *Religion* as a social goal as a consequence of his introduction in this work of the concept of *radical evil.* In
this work, radical evil is defined by Kant as an impediment infecting
the social condition of man, who, regardless of his civil sophistication,
remains in an ethical state of nature. I will first explicate the relationship between radical evil and the predisposition to humanity from
which the ordinary condition of social conflict arises. I will then attempt
to demonstrate the problems that radical evil creates for an "individualistic" model of moral perfection. I will claim that the theme that
connects the duty of individual moral perfection to the duty to promote an ideal social union is the problem of the inconstancy of the
moral disposition in an ethical state of nature. The ethical commonwealth is the ideal that individuals must propose to one another as
the means for overcoming the ethical state of nature.

3

Radical Evil and the Ethical Commonwealth

The ethical commonwealth is the central theme of book 3 of Kant's *Religion*. The introduction of this concept is preceded by an analysis of the "ethical state of nature" in terms that reintroduce the concept of radical evil. The discussion of the ethical state of nature prevailing within civil society parallels the discussion of the corruption of the predisposition to humanity in book 1. In both contexts evil is viewed as a positive impediment and not as the mere absence of virtue.[1] In both contexts Kant relates the power of "evil" to the social condition of mankind. In book 3 Kant maintains that the obstacles to the attainment of a stable disposition toward virtue do not arise from our physical nature per se (neither from our needs nor our passions). Impediments to virtue arise from our social inclinations, from our very relatedness to others, which occasions anxiety and insecurity. Kant writes: "Envy, the lust for power, greed, and the malignant inclinations bound up with these, besiege his nature, contented within itself as soon as he is among men."[2]

Apparently, the predisposition to the good, which is an original endowment of each individual, will not suffice to ensure a universal social harmony. The existence of others, the inescapable social condition of man, will create challenges for the moral life. Kant's concept of an ethical commonwealth is posited as a necessary ideal in the context of a moral need for a harmonization of dispositions. Kant maintains that we have a "moral need" arising from our own obligation to pursue the moral life, to seek this harmonization of dispositions. What can this mean?

This moral need arises from Kant's introduction in book 1 of the propensity to evil as a characteristic of the human will. That the attainment of virtue must take the form of efforts to create a more perfect social union is a consequence of the relation of this propensity to the predisposition to humanity. Because the predisposition to humanity is the ground of our social nature, the corruption of this ground will transform the task of moral perfection for the individual. If virtue is connected with the restoration of the proper ends of our social nature, then the resulting duty, to promote the ideal of a virtuous social union is inseparable from the goal of individual moral perfection. The concept of radical evil is systematically connected to Kant's general moral philosophy by generating a specifically social content and purposive character for the idea of the highest good in the form of the ethical commonwealth. Unlike the kingdom of ends introduced in the *Groundwork*, the ethical commonwealth is associated with the historical development of particular ethical communities in the public domain. Kant's analysis of the universal character of the problem of evil shapes the historical content of the highest good. In order to clarify the claim that the ethical commonwealth represents Kant's model of the highest good, and further to demonstrate the basis of the moral obligation to promote this ideal, it will be necessary to retrace Kant's development in book 1 of the *Religion* of the concept of the propensity to evil.

It is well known that Kant claims in book 1 that the propensity to evil is universally ascribable to man as man. There is, however, little agreement as to how this "universality" is to be understood. Is it merely an empirical generalization from experience useful in guiding our anthropological investigations? Some of Kant's statements support this line of reasoning, but others clearly imply more than this. For instance, although Kant states that evil is not derivable from the concept of man in general and is hence not formally necessary, he also claims that evil is subjectively necessary to every man, "even the best."

Kant's distinction between formal necessity and subjective necessity appears to parallel his distinction between the finite rational will as such and the specifically human will, which includes particular human predispositions. Since evil does not arise from the finite rational will (*Willkur*) as such, it is compatible with the faculty of freedom. We can be both evil and free. If, however, evil is subjectively necessary to every man, it must be bound up with specifically human predispositions that can be affected by the exercise of freedom. As Gordon E. Michalson Jr. expresses the dilemma:

> Kant must walk a fine line between attributing moral evil
> to something naturally given in human nature and attributing

it to some force or capacity utterly irrelevant to basic human nature. The purpose of the vocabulary of predispositions and propensity is to enable him to walk this fine line.[3]

In book 1 of the *Religion* Kant outlines three predispositions that he claims are "elements in the fixed character and destiny of man."[4] These are animality, humanity, and personality. All three predispositions are said to be bound up with the exercise of the will and hence presumably can be modified and directed by reason (purposive causality), although none can be "extirpated."

The predisposition to animality is bound up with our physical needs and thus arises from characteristics that we may have in common with nonrational beings. The predisposition to personality is simply our receptivity to the moral law, our capacity for respect for reason, which, while it may remain unexpressed or suppressed by our preference for other incentives, cannot be used contrary to its purpose. It is the second predisposition, the predisposition to humanity, that is most closely related to Kant's concept of evil.

Kant claims that the propensity to evil is "rooted in humanity itself."[5] Although he does not make the connection between this propensity and the predisposition to humanity explicit, the universality of Kant's ascription suggests a process whereby this original predisposition is corrupted or used contrary to its purpose. The corrupt element must be something fundamental, something basic to our mode of being. The predisposition to humanity, unlike the predisposition to animality, presupposes the exercise of reason, and specifically a reason that compares. The "self-love" that arises from this predisposition is not a mechanical self-preservation. It is here that conscious reflection on our purposes can begin. And it is significant that this form of reflection involves a reason that recognizes and compares the purposes of self and other. Even the basic desires bound up with this predisposition, desires for equality and esteem, are ascribable only to beings who create a dimension of their nature through social interaction. Thus, the predisposition to humanity represents the basis of the social and cultural dimension of human nature, the dimension through which freedom will historically develop. Human history will take its bearings from the manner in which this predisposition is shaped and developed. Further articulating the function of the concept of a predisposition, Michalson notes:

> The term "predisposition" is Kant's way of talking about basic human nature as it is prior to any actual exercise of freedom. We are not "really" what we essentially are until we exercise

our freedom. . . . But surely we are something prior to that point, and the notion of an original predisposition enables Kant to map out what that is.[6]

Kant maintains that the predisposition to humanity is the original basis of the rational principle of self-love. The fundamental desire associated with this predisposition is the desire for equality. This desire clearly springs from our rational–moral nature, but also from a reason that measures and compares. In its corrupt form this desire becomes an inclination "to acquire worth in the opinion of others."[7] While recognition of the self and others as moral beings, as rational "subjects" or "ends," is implicit in the idea of equality, moral recognition is a practical judgment, not a merely logical deduction. The moral bond between people is something to be created, and moral recognition requires specific affirmative acts. When the "self" withholds this affirmation, we are oriented toward others only insofar as they promote our worth; we are interested in the ends of others only to the degree that they serve our purposes.

The predisposition toward humanity is a predisposition toward the good in that it posits the self as intrinsically related to others in a potential moral community. It thereby poses the moral task of the integration of ends. But unless the desires for equality and esteem are conditioned by an affirmation of the intrinsic value of others, this predisposition becomes the source of jealousy and rivalry, from which arise a multitude of "vices of culture." Thus, while the predisposition to humanity begins as the basis of particular incentives, it is also the locus of the general principle of self-love that Kant later explicitly identifies with the ground of the propensity to evil. Evil, then, is not an additional constituent of human nature but a particular transformation of self-love in a social context.[8] My interpretation of radical evil, unlike others such as Michalson's,[9] makes a strong connection between evil and our social condition. The strength of my interpretation is that it can shed light on the moral significance of the transformation of social–cultural institutions and on the role of the ethical commonwealth in Kant's philosophy of history. If this interpretation is correct, then Kant's statement that the propensity to evil is "rooted in humanity itself" is something more than a catchy phrase. There is an intrinsic connection between the "social inclinations" and the propensity to evil. While Kant's general indebtedness to Rousseau is often recognized, it is also frequently asserted that unlike Rousseau, Kant maintains that evil is not a result of social institutions but is a characteristic inherent within individuals for which they can be held accountable. But these two perspectives are not necessarily incompatible once we accept that social institutions arise from human interaction and that social inclinations are part of the natural constitution of individuals. Individuals can be held accountable for their participation in social systems. The real difference is that for Rousseau, unlike Kant, freedom has no transcendental location and, because of its association with natural independence, declines with the development of social inclinations.

If we examine closely what Kant says concerning the nature of moral evil we shall find this connection confirmed. The propensity to evil, in its most essential meaning, is an impurity in maxims. The moral law presents itself to the human will as a sufficient incentive and as the supreme condition of all other ends. The moral law, then, as pure practical reason, dictates that the ends of the self be formed in conformity with a "system of ends." This dictate commands an orientation toward others whereby our ends are systematically integrated with the ends of others. Since no motivating ground can become an "incentive" for the human will unless and until it is taken up into a "maxim" (a subjective ground of action), the moral law must be actively adopted. If the moral law were the only motivating ground possible for the will, the human condition would be spontaneously socially integrated as if "by nature."

However, in forming the "highest" or supreme maxim the human will according to Kant, naturally incorporates both self–love and the moral law as incentives. As previously noted, self–love is formulated by a comparative reason that measures the worth of self in relation to others. While the moral law would have us regard each self as being of unconditioned worth (dignity is an inherently moral attribute) and would have each intend an integration of ends, self–love motivates each to attempt the subordination of the ends of others so as to enhance individual "worth" in the marketplace of opinion.

While human beings are not accountable for the existence of self–love as a motivating ground, they are accountable for adopting self–love as a dominant incentive. Since either the incentive of self–love or the moral law is sufficient to determine the will, the fundamental character of the will depends upon the priority assigned these diverse incentives, that is, which is made the condition of the other.

The propensity to resist the moral law as a sufficient incentive and to rely on the incentive of self–love becomes morally culpable insofar as the incentive of the moral law becomes subordinated to the incentive of self–love. The evil that is the radical "flaw" in human nature and from which many diverse and sometimes malicious vices arise is not a flagrant rejection of the moral law per se. Kant denies that outright rejection of the moral law is possible for a human will. And neither would the objectives of self-love require it. The form of law that practical reason provides can be used instrumentally to unify the ends of individuals and to formulate the pragmatic policies that enable us to take advantage of our associations with others. Self-love most often takes the form of the prudential advancement of self-interest through accepted social practice. Historically, accepted social practices often arise from coalitions of power formed for mutual benefit. Unfortunately, these pragmatic coalitions often fall short of the moral ideal of the systematic integration of ends. Kant reminds us that we are very likely to say, without detecting any contradiction, that a good man is one who is "evil in a way common to all."[10] Thus, merely lawful actions, as many moral philosophers have lamented, may lead only to a minimal morality falling short of substantive moral ideals.

Moral evil is the consequence of a radical choice between basic incentives that structure the human will. Because this choice informs all further free action, we cannot go any further in our explanations. We have reached the ultimate "condition of the possibility" of particular actions, the transcendental realm. The choice or "supreme act" through which the moral disposition or "intelligible character" is formed is an expression of transcendental freedom. Transcendental freedom is possible only because an aspect of practical reason (Wille) is pure or unconditioned by the sensuous world. Yet in the process whereby this freedom is exercised (Willkur) and the highest maxim articulated, reason can be utilized as an instrument for the attainment of the specific and narrowly (privately) conceived ends of the phenomenal self.[11] It is in the manner in which the self is conceived and constituted that the corruption of the will takes place and evil arises. Any account of Kant's concept of the self that posits a simple dualism of rational versus physical nature would render evil a consequence of the existence of our physical nature. This Kant denies. Even the inclusion of a fundamental "choice" between these incentives, the model of evil as an orientation toward the physical world, would make it difficult to distinguish weakness of will from physical determination. I maintain that Kant's vision of evil in the Religion is actually more complex than a dual-nature-plus-choice model could explain. The triadic structure of human nature presented through the predispositions includes a social dimension that is neither purely physical nor purely rational. Through the predisposition to humanity, material objects of desire, the elements of the shifting ideal of happiness, are culturally constructed and infused with social significance. Thus, it can be argued that the propensity to evil as articulated in the Religion is a corruption of one's humanity and the human-social condition. The general principle of self-love, which Kant explicitly relates to the propensity to evil, arises from the predisposition to humanity insofar as the self asserts its own ends as the condition of the recognition of the value of others. In withholding affirmation of their ends and constructing the value of others as conditional, we construct other selves as "mere means" and in the process instrumentalize our own reason. It is in the "objectification" of others—and through others, ourselves—that the debasement of our humanity occurs. It is not the mere force of the external world nor the raw attractiveness of material objects that underlies the subversion of the moral law.

Since, however, according to Kant, man is essentially characterized by freedom, even as a natural being man is not immediately subject to mechanical determination. And despite our immoral intent, the self can never become a mere object. Nature is, as it were, a stepmother who will not immediately accommodate our desires. The satisfaction of human desires requires the development of reason which is never perfected in the individual. It is reason that first bestows upon us our social nature and leads us to compare ourselves with others. The propensity to evil is identified with the principle of self-love not insofar as the self is an animal being with physical needs but insofar as the self is a social being that seeks the recognition of others yet refuses to acknowledge the intrinsic value of others. Insofar as pure reason is an incentive, it operates to restrict and condition the nature of our desires, making an integration of ends possible. Reason is the only power capable of integrating our total nature, because that nature is intersubjectively constituted.

One can view this detachment of the self from the incentive of pure reason seeking this integration as a kind of "transcendental fall" that individuals reenact as they assume their social roles and freely enter into the power struggles of everyday life. This is the individual or top-down perspective. But one can also view evil from the bottom up, as innate to the species, insofar as the ordinary social condition is the focus of a fundamental moral task, the creation of an ethical community. Viewed in this latter way, there are no "private" solutions to the problem of evil, because the transformation of our social conditions is an inherently collective effort.

Given Kant's analysis of the nature of the corruption of the predisposition to humanity, one would have to conclude that the individual desiring to transform his or her corrupt disposition could not begin this process or attain to moral perfection alone. What is at stake is not the fulfillment of virtue in the sense of good deeds, which can be motivated by the desire to demonstrate our "superiority" (and which Kant claims can often be attributed to mere good fortune). Action in accordance with the moral law, empirically good character, is fully compatible with the continued dominance of the principle of self-love. Virtue clearly goes beyond good deeds. What is at stake is a reorientation of the self, a positive act of identification with others, which moves beyond the ordinary social condition. This reorientation is, of course, itself a radical act, a moral revolution, but it is mediated by a reflective projection of the ethical commonwealth that provides it with a purposive and social content.

While this analysis goes some way toward demonstrating the social dimensions of moral evil, one might say that what has not been fully addressed is the "subjective necessity" of evil. Granted, individuals who have subordinated the moral law to the incentive of self-love face the further difficulty of being continuously challenged by the presence of others whose dispositions are similarly corrupt. How does this prove that some individuals do not stand outside this influence by virtue of their initial commitment to the moral law? Or how does this prove that some individuals may not break away through a successful "individual revolution"?

There is no direct "proof" that completely virtuous individuals do not exist or that they cannot sustain a successful moral revolution alone. The only type of access we can have to the question of the individual disposition is by way of inference from the general course of a person's life. However, the question of the way in which we view the disposition is itself a matter of practical importance affecting moral conduct. That is why Kant distinguishes in the *Religion* between questions of moral dogmatics and questions of moral discipline. Starting with the fact that the moral law is apprehended as an unconditioned incentive and a motivating force, Kant maintains that absence of goodness is possible only as a consequence of a real and contrary determination of the will.[12] Moral theorizing attempts to demonstrate what must be the case from a transcendental perspective for evil to be possible. We can theorize the conditions that make evil possible only as an inference from life conduct. But given the compatibility of evil and conformity to law, we cannot assume a good disposition simply from good conduct. Things are different, though, when we attempt to pass judgment on conduct that fails to conform to morality. Though a particular judgment that the action of another is evil can be in error, we must infer a corrupt disposition as a condition of the possibility of any conduct that we consider to be culpably evil. Thus, the possibility of judgments of moral culpability rests upon tracing evil back to a corrupt disposition. We ultimately face an even more serious question when we ask how we ought to regard our own conduct. We have no privileged access to our own disposition, and while we may wish to "humbug" ourselves as to our own deficiencies, Kant's rigorism with respect to the definition of the moral disposition reaches deep. The disposition as such can only be good or evil, and as the conditions of the exercise of our freedom are the shared conditions of social existence, we have no reason to apply different standards to others and to self. The world must be as a mirror to our souls. Moral self-doubt completes the circle.

Therefore if evil exists, if we are moved to protest its existence, we must suspect its power is pervasive. The standpoint of moral discipline requires that we view ourselves in light of our imperfections. If we exempt ourselves from this judgment we risk self-deception and the loss of the power to combat the propensity to evil. Although Kant's universalization of evil may be discouraging when viewed from an individual perspective, the radicalness of evil opens insights into levels of social interconnectedness that can in turn offer new avenues to freedom. Evil is generally viewed as a corruption pertaining to the isolated individual whose sole hope lies in an external, nonhuman source of aid. But once evil is viewed as embedded in our social condition, neither the problem nor the solution is adequately addressed in this way.

While what we attempt to do toward the breaking of this "power" of evil cannot help us as long as it is focused upon our own individual predicament (because that merely reinforces self-love or the propensity to evil), by focusing on virtue as a social good we can transform the conditions that constrain us. Focusing upon only the "purity" of own intentions is a bit of moral fetishism. Furthermore, we cannot know intentions independently of our purposes. Transformation of our social conditions must begin with reflection on the nature of a moral world. We must imagine how our actions can purposively shape this world. But can we know what purposes fit a moral world? Can we know when our actions actually further these purposes and when they do not? The first question is in part addressed by the role of the ethical commonwealth as a reflective end. The second question concerns the function of moral "hope" in providing a context within which individual action is supported by its place in a larger community. The fragmentation of human activity requires conceptualization in terms of ideal projects that are the work of a universal community. Hope goes beyond the cognitive warrant provided by judgments of purposiveness concerning individual actions in connecting these with the grounds on which the very possibility of a universal community depends. While moral hope in a narrow sense is the bridge to Kant's conception of religious "faith," it has ramifications, which I will attempt to demonstrate further in later chapters, for the entire philosophy of history. If the ethical commonwealth is a truly universal community then its ultimate foundations will be religious, although not in a narrowly ecclesiastical sense.

I will attempt now to demonstrate why an analysis of the moral life that begins with the particular acts of individuals must ultimately lead to a recognition of the moral need for ethical community. The limits inherent in the analysis of the particular actions of the individual arise from a combination of epistemological and moral considerations. This leads Kant to an exposition of what unifies and provides a basis for the moral judgment of individual character. But in analyzing the intelligible disposition in book 1 of the *Religion*, as we have seen, Kant quickly shifts his subject from that of an individual to that of the species. In analyzing the role of natural predispositions and their relationship to the propensity to evil, Kant is operating at a transcendental level. The very constraints involved in analyzing the nature of the fundamental disposition require that Kant begin his examination of the intelligible disposition at a generic level. Allen Wood refers to Kant's procedure in the *Religion* as "the critique of man's moral nature." He writes: "Kant attempts to answer these questions through an investigation which is critical in character, in that it aims at human self-knowledge obtained systematically by means of an examination of the "sources, extent and limits" of human capacities.[13]

From the outset, Kant explicitly maintains that the "subject" of this discourse is not the "particular individual" but the "entire species." He repeatedly notes that in analyzing the fundamental attributes of human volition he is describing the human condition and is not thereby inferring his concepts from particular actions nor deducing anything concerning a particular individual.

As we noted, Kant begins book 1 of the *Religion* (as he did part 1 of the *Groundwork*) with a consideration of the implications of "ordinary judgment." And there appears to be resounding agreement: Evil exists. One cannot, of course, with respect to particular actions judge directly the nature of their intelligible ground from their apparent "rightness" or "wrongness." Unless connected to a principle or pattern of activity, particular actions are mere appearances. But even taken as patterns, right actions and actions that do not conform to morality do not provide the same type of "evidence" for the existence of a disposition. This is because, according to Kant, actions that conform to law can, across all cases, admit of a derivation from a nonmoral incentive. Self-love is perfectly capable of setting us on the course of right action. Therefore the connection between right action and a moral incentive is always hypothetical even when right action is a consistent pattern of behavior, whereas the connection between any wrong action and the existence of a "counterincentive" is direct. For if a person who can recognize the moral law is capable of acting contrary to the law, then that person can only do so if an incentive contrary to the moral law is effectively operative. And such an individual can only be accountable for these unlawful actions through some attribute of his or her free will. Therefore if evil can in any case be attributable to a free being, it can be so imputed only by virtue of a characteristic inherent to that freedom. Thus it appears that if moral evil is not an "illusion"—that is, if evil is possible for any free being—it must be possible for every free being. Evil, then, is not so much a characteristic of Tom, Dick, or Harry as it is a characteristic of our fundamental capacity for choice. The existence of any evil is evidence of our universal vulnerability. Kant defends the character of this transcendental but "universal" judgment in these words: "Because this character concerns a relation of the will, which is free (and the concept of which is therefore not empirical), to the moral law as an incentive(the concept of which, likewise, is purely intellectual), it must be apprehended a priori through the concept of evil, so far as evil is possible under the laws of freedom (of obligation and accountability)."[14]

If, then the individual's right to assume that he or she is in possession of a good will (disposition) is at best always questionable, moral self-certainty is not a recommendable moral attitude and is for Kant akin to self-deception. We have seen that from the perspective of a systematic and critical investigation of the human disposition, Kant has adduced good reasons for the admission or postulation of a universal propensity to evil. But what difference does the admission of such a propensity make to the moral life of the individual? Does not the individual retain the same set of duties/obligations regardless of the existence of an innate tendency to transgression? Kant's explanation of the function of this postulate in our moral reasoning, as we have noted, involves his familiar appeal to "two standpoints."

From the "standpoint" of moral dogmatics, the assumption of such a propensity makes no difference. It does not invalidate the moral law nor eliminate our receptivity to it. We cannot lose the moral incentive, for if we did it could never be regained and the conditions for moral accountability would cease to obtain. But Kant maintains that from the "standpoint" of moral discipline, this assumption makes a marked difference, for it tells us

We cannot start from an innocence natural to us . . . we must begin with the incessant counteraction against it. Since this leads only to a progress, endlessly continuing . . . it follows that the conversion of the disposition . . . is to be found in the change of the highest inward ground.[15]

The standpoint of moral discipline is rooted in the empirical character and as such is necessarily temporal. But as shaped by the consciousness of our liability to transgression, the "object" of our moral judgment is transformed. Our actions are regarded under the idea of a possible progress. Our concern shifts from the face-value of independent actions to the principle of their connectedness. And we are concerned with a "quality of the whole" in terms of which the series can be regarded as an "act of restoration." This quality of the whole is evidence of a "revolution," or what Kant has called "the change of the highest inward ground." Since it is our life "as a whole" that is the subject of this analysis, the transformation that is attributed to the disposition does not entail any sudden or abrupt change in the empirical character. For no part stands for the whole; each draws its moral quality from a course of development. From within the temporal perspective, we must view the abandonment of evil and the entrance into goodness as "simultaneously and continuously" occurring and as therefore never complete in time. Even ups and downs can be admitted into a pattern of moral improvement. We can view each day as a new beginning as long as our life as a whole, and not just good deeds, is the moral objective.

Kant concludes that his "two standpoints" are not contradictory; the postulation of this propensity is not opposed to the "possibility of this restoration." Yet there remains a troublesome residue. For would a simple reversal of these incentives be adequate to the original claim of the moral law to be the sole, as well as the sufficient, incentive for our will? Did not the propensity to evil, which Kant maintains ought to be viewed as acquired (though not in time), enter as our own fault? If this original offense can never be removed, can anything less than its eradication count as restitution? By Kant's own admission, that is not within our power. The propensity to evil, we recall, is "subjectively necessary to every man, even the best."

In discussing the issue of irremediable guilt arising from the existence of this propensity, Kant makes use of concepts drawn from the practical postulates of the immortality of the soul and the existence of God. Nonetheless, the "hope" generated by these postulates is always qualified as conditioned by our "own" efforts. But because it is not within our own power to break the hold of this propensity even when the reversal of incentives is granted, the "perilousness" of the human condition remains unchanged even by the theoretical possibility of individual salvation.

Given the depths of the problem he has uncovered, Kant cannot leave his analysis of the nature of vice and virtue with the "individual's" predicament. The struggle with which the moral life is engaged is with "principalities and powers," and the individual is not, as it were, the ultimate frontier, but rather a participant in a larger drama that concerns the human destiny. In book 3 of the *Religion*, Kant presses on to investigate the social context of this struggle. What this analysis reveals about the nature of vice and virtue significantly recasts the terms in which we must think about the "moral life " and the nature of the "highest good."

Although we have been analyzing this propensity as it might inhere in a particular subject, we recall that Kant maintains that the reasons we have for attributing such a propensity to any given subject are the same reasons for ascribing this to all human agents. This extension has important consequences for the way in which the individual must conceive the possibility of the "moral revolution." The idea of a moral life must include not only the unification of all of one's own acts/maxims but also an essential connection of these to the acts/maxims of other moral subjects. In other words, given the universality of the ascription of this propensity, the "moral life" must be represented as a social or collective undertaking. Thus the "moral revolution" cannot be a purely private, contentless act. Although not a "particular" action in the empirical realm, this moral revolution, like all human action, must entail a purpose; and, given the nature of the problem of overcoming evil, that purpose or goal must be one that is social in significance. In the course of clarifying the meaning of this necessary object or final end, the social significance of the theistic postulate will become apparent.

In book 3 of the *Religion*, subtitled "The Victory of the Good Principle over the Evil Principle, and the Founding of a Kingdom of God on Earth," Kant notes that the "highest prize" that the morally well disposed individual can attain by virtue of his continuous struggle to reform his own disposition is to "be free from bondage," a negative form of freedom that cannot, however, protect him from moral backsliding. When he reflects upon the circumstances that expose him to this danger, he must include in these reflections the quality of his relationships with others. We recall that Kant presents a Rousseauean analysis of the human condition in which he notes that it is not because of one's individual nature and "original needs" that one becomes inclined toward evil. The passions that disturb our original predisposition to the good are evoked by the mere presence of others. Kant states:

> Envy, the lust for power, greed, and the malignant inclinations bound up with these, besiege his nature, contented within itself, as soon as he is among men. And it is not even necessary

to assume that these are men sunk in evil and examples to lead him astray; it suffices that they are at hand, that they surround him, and that they are men, for them mutually to corrupt each other's predispositions and make one another evil.[16]

These provocative remarks have been prepared for by Kant's presentation of the predisposition to humanity in book 1, where he noted that our original and apparently "innocent" self-love is rooted in a "reason which compares"; it inclines us to human society and is intended by nature to be our "spur to culture." Even our ideas of happiness, which provide the driving contents of self-love, are rooted in this comparative reason, for "we judge ourselves happy or unhappy only by making comparisons with others."[17] Thus, what we received from nature as a self-love originally limited to "need" becomes through the exercise of freedom, in the context of human culture, an expanding system of social desires.

The preference we display for these "acquired desires" is the very formula of the propensity to evil, which apparently includes our entire social-cultural being and is in this sense "entwined with" and "rooted in" our humanity. The propensity to evil is not something that is simply "within me" and "within you," but something that operates within our very mode of association. Thus Kant implies that our hope to effect a revolution "within" rests upon the transformation of the social conditions of our existence. Models of moral perfection that view the achievement of virtue as a result of private decision making concerned only with the "purity" of intention and detached from all purposes are rendered by Kant's view of the human condition in the *Religion* "futile." To maintain such a posture is to remain in an "ethical state of nature," which Kant defines as "one in which the good principle, which resides in each man, is continuously attacked by the evil which is found in him and also in everyone else."[18]

Now Kant takes up the social significance of the propensity to evil quite explicitly and draws from this predicament the conclusion that unless individuals deliberately unite into a society "for the sake of the laws of virtue," they cannot hope to remain free from bondage. Kant writes:

If no means can be discovered for the forming of an alliance uniquely designed as a protection against this evil . . . this association with others would keep man, however much, as a single individual, he may have done to throw off the sovereignty of evil, incessantly in danger of falling back under its dominion.[19]

This is a very challenging statement, for it reaffirms the limited and negative character of the "freedom from," which is all that the unaided individual can attain. Such is not yet freedom in its positive signification of a power to live in righteousness. The latter depends upon the individual's submission to common principles of virtue that unite the dispositions. One could reduce the twists and turns in Kant's analysis to the following: since the commitment to virtue requires the abandonment of the "ethical state of nature," one has a moral obligation to enter into and promote the ethical commonwealth.

The idea of a social union is, of course, not an entirely new development, for in the *Groundwork* Kant links the idea of universal legislation to the status of the legislator as a member of a "realm of ends." Kant writes:

> Reason then relates every maxim of the will as legislating universally to every other will. . . . Morality consists in the reference of all actions to the making of laws by which alone a realm of ends is possible.[20]

At the heart of this "realm" is the idea of a colegislation from which a harmony of maxims or "whole of ends" is expected to result. Although the realization of such a system is conditioned upon everyone adhering to "common laws," these laws are conceived as arising from "disregarding the personal differences of rational beings and all particular contents of their private ends."[21]

The underlying paradigm is one of individual moral self-sufficiency. If each individual "reformed" his or her "own" nature, abstracting from the particular and private, a systematic harmony of dispositions would automatically result. Good dispositions are naturally in harmony, and there can be no conflict between them. This position appears to be revised in the *Religion,* in which Kant tells us that good wills not united under common principles of virtue will "recede, through their dissension, from the common goal of goodness."[22] There is also a notable difference in the *Groundwork* in the role of the theistic postulate. Even if the kingdom of ends were thought of as united under a sovereign, this would not add anything essentially different to the constitution of that realm. The relationship of the sovereign to each member is "external" and mediated only by the recognition of that virtue which is in and for itself "complete" in each individual. The idea of the sovereign in the kingdom of ends appears primarily useful as a limiting concept. The sovereign is that member who is "without wants and of unlimited capabilities."[23] But the internal essence or constitution of the realm is not changed by the existence of the sovereign.

In the *Religion* one finds a different, clearly constitutive relationship between the idea of God and the ethical commonwealth. The
unity of the ethical commonwealth and the purity of its principles are
viewed as derived from the holiness of the will that serves as its "foundation." Prior to the *Religion*, the primary role of God in Kant's moral
philosophy was to allocate happiness, proportioned to virtue, either
directly in the next life or indirectly by coaxing nature into agreement
with moral volition. This purely supplementary role is a consequence
of two suppositions that are discarded in the *Religion*. The first is that
the individual can adequately achieve virtue by the exertion of his or
her own moral capacities alone. The second is that the desire for happiness has independent roots in nature that necessarily limit the
achievement of the complete or highest good.

The introduction of a propensity to evil in book 1 of the *Religion*
alters both assumptions. The striving for virtue is given an interper-
sonal orientation and end. And particular desires, drawing their significance from our social and cultural condition, are rooted in volition.
Nature per se is no longer the targeted culprit. The hindrances to the
realization of the highest good are located in the nexus of human
relationships. The centrality of the theme of mutual engagement leads
Kant to the explicit formulation of the highest good as a social goal. In
referring to this "social good," Kant stipulates that it cannot be achieved
by the "exertions of the single individual toward his own perfection."[24]

Now, it obviously follows from the characterization of the goal as
social that it refers to more than the single individual. But equal emphasis must be placed on the nature of the "perfection" sought, for this
is not a mere aggregate of private perfections as the model of individual moral self-sufficiency would suggest. The ethical commonwealth,
Kant writes, "requires rather a union of such individuals into a whole
toward the same goal—into a system of well-disposed men, in which
and through whose unity alone the highest moral good can come to
pass."[25]

Unlike the kingdom of ends, this union cannot properly be represented as arising from the "good will," since it is the will striving to
become good that falls under this obligation and morally needs this
union. While the obligation to enter into such a union is of a totally
unique kind, it has the force of duty, for the moral life literally hinges
upon it. The obligation to promote this goal in effect subsumes the
individual's striving toward personal perfection and provides it with
social content. The commitment to the highest good then provides the
disposition with the unique focus it requires. It is with respect to this
commitment that the moral meaning of the postulate of God's existence is finally fully clarified. Kant writes: "[T]his duty will require the

presupposition of another idea, namely, that of a higher moral Being, through whose universal dispensation the forces of separate individuals, insufficient in themselves, are united for a common end."[26]

The unity of the ethical commonwealth is more complex than the abstract unification of the kingdom of ends. The purposive striving of individuals to create conditions that will make virtue possible not merely for themselves but for the entire species transcends the individual's capacity to clearly envision the outcomes. We must intend more than we can grasp or control. In "Evil and the Moral Power of God," Philip Rossi argues that in developing an account of the highest good in terms of the social destiny of the human race, Kant is required to provide a more complex account of the relationship between good and evil than found in the *Groundwork*. Rossi notes that "Actions must now be classified in terms of their bearing on the attainment of this social and historical destiny of the human species as well as in terms of their marking the good will of agents."[27]

Clearly Kant does not regard the attainment of this social goal to be a straightforward function of the "conscientiousness " of agents. As Rossi notes, the intended good can "misfire" or fail to have effects that succeed in promoting the highest good. If we review what Kant actually says concerning this perplexing possibility, we find that he does not make any reference to the intractability of nature, as he was earlier inclined to do. In the *Religion*, Kant's concern is consistently focused on what goes on within volition that thwarts this ideal. Or more properly, given what I take to be Kant's expanded understanding of what counts as internal to volition, he focuses on what goes on between moral agents. Intending-the-good is accompanied by a residual reservation that weakens mutual commitment. Kant writes: "[D]espite the good will of each individual, yet, because they lack a principle which unites them, they recede, through their dissension, from the common goal of goodness and, just as though they were instruments of evil, expose one another to the risk of falling once again under the sovereignty of the evil principle."[28]

Although expressed as a spatial metaphor, this passage indicates a form of moral distance between moral subjects that must be overcome. The essentially private sphere of intention must take a public form of communication, a public pledge of "common allegiance" to principles derived from an unchangeable or holy will. That is to say moral laws are now also viewed as "divine commands" constitutive of a particular form of community—namely, an ethical community.

It appears to be Kant's view that when the moral life is conscientiously pursued, the "moral need" for such a union is undeniable. Moreover, this need reveals itself to be a need we "share" with each other.

Each member being insufficient to stand assurance of his or her pledge must think or presuppose the existence of a perfect moral being through whom we are bonded each to each. The idea of a moral governor is the correlate of the "We" that the human community requires as the condition of individual moral perfection. In "Autonomy and Community," Rossi comments that "Although the attainment of an abiding 'we' is the end to which our freedom is ordered, the very exercise of our freedom makes manifest the inability of our freedom to give us surety of the attainment of this end."[29]

Rossi concludes that it is through the endeavor to create this community that we "become open to be touched by the power of God's transcendence."[30] I would add that it is by way of tracking our mutual engagement in the very condition of moral failure from which we all begin that Kant roots the moral need for shared faith. And from shared faith arises the mutual empowerment that makes the highest good possible.

The ethical commonwealth is defined in terms of mutuality and integration, which constitute a social good transcending a mere aggregate of individual goods. Kant writes that such a good cannot be achieved by the individual aiming at his or her "own perfection." Because the highest moral good cannot be achieved merely by the exertions of the single individual toward his or her own moral perfection but requires rather a union of such individuals into a whole, it seems to me that commentators who attempt to reduce Kant's conception of virtue to individual "purity" of the will are mistaken. In the *Religion*, both the character of the highest good and the role of God undergo a transformation that reinforces the social orientation of moral development. While nothing external to the will can be the source of the required unity, we have also noted how the very imperfections of the human will render human activity per se an inadequate ground of a "social union." However much I recognize the need for a social union to be a condition of overcoming the rivalry that hinders morality, the response of the other to me is something that I can neither control nor be indifferent to. The other is equally dependent upon assurances that I am in no-condition to provide. It appears, then, that the original condition of a "free" finite rational being is necessarily an "ethical state of nature," despite the marks we bear of membership in a moral community.

That ethical community is something that we must enter into entails public–social action with its pledge to the laws of virtue. But the enduring subjective "we" is something that unaided individuals cannot create. Since the issue of ethical commitment concerns the disposition and not the external conformity that creates political union, the supplement of external force cannot bridge the gap. Nor can any cultural or social institution provide an adequate ground. We must move from acknowledging the depths of our common need to acknowledging our common dependence upon a *source of moral unification* whose purity and constancy is beyond question. Shared moral faith is the requisite bond. The object of this moral faith is not God envisioned as the physical author of nature and bending its laws so as to mechanically supplement virtue. The objection that such a God is an ad hoc regulator of a poorly designed system is well founded. It is rather God as Absolute Person, through whose continuous presence the moral law abides while our commitments waver, who is the necessary object of this moral faith. Even if we are intelligible or rational beings, this absolute continuity in moral commitment is not something that we can guarantee from our own resources.[31] The God of the *Religion* functions less as an ad hoc regulator of the material world and more as the Moral Bondsman of a universal and enduring community.

In the *Opus Postum*, according to Webb, Kant explicates the idea of God as that of a "moral relation within me" and as the "totality of Practical Reason,"[32] which indicates again the primary role of God in providing a ground of moral relationships, a source and font of moral community. Michalson views this strange language as Kant's attempt to downplay God as an entity separate from ourselves and to "divinize reason."[33] If, however, we assume the perspective of the ethical commonwealth, moral community depends upon more than the distributed function of the moral law operating individually. And it is not enough that there be in addition a Divine Entity in a completely transcendent sense. Moral community requires for its completion an immanent ground of moral relationship. Martin Buber's view, although more poetic, strikes me as similar in spirit. According to Buber, the I–Thou relationship is not simply an internal relationship of the individual to God but is also the ground and condition of all human and social relationships.[34]

Thus, I must disagree with commentators such as Van der Linden and Yovel who claim that Kant has no special argument for the postulate of God's existence other than the appeal to an ontological "Something" that guarantees that nature is responsive to our efforts. The ground of the ethical commonwealth must be a moral person. While some commentators, including Van der Linden, appropriately focus on the moral community as the historical human expression of the highest good, few, other than Rossi, integrate Kant's concept of moral evil into their conceptions of the hindrances to our endeavors. And once these hindrances are understood to be internal to the human will, the form of aid must be capable of operating internally as well. It is then not a matter of indifference how we conceive this necessary supplement. Faith is "rational," according to Kant when our conception, although going beyond what we can intuit, responds to a genuine need of reason. Faith then provides a necessary "orientation" in thinking and a ground of hope that our actions can fulfill our purposes.[35]

While Van der Linden concedes that this "hope"—which he recognizes must accompany an ongoing moral commitment—may become unstable and may therefore be supported by faith, he does not acknowledge the manner in which the existence of a propensity to evil within the human disposition changes the dimensions of the challenge to the human capacity to achieve the highest good.[36] Thus while many socially oriented commentators attempt to provide communitarian applications for a Kantian ethic, their commitment to a secular foundation and their dismissal of the conception of radical evil make it difficult to provide a universal social and historical scope for their projects. That the highest good is intended by Kant to be a universal social good is nowhere more strongly asserted than in the *Religion*. Yet this is clearly consequent to his view of evil as likewise universally internal to human interaction. It is of central significance to the systematic character of Kantian ethics that Kant does not assert the social character of the good as independent of our struggle to overcome moral imperfection, but precisely in the context of that problem. If this ideal community is to be viewed as a universal moral project and the object of a constant historical endeavor, then the "something" than sustains it must have the requisite moral and intentional attributes of a person. If the ethical commonwealth is the highest good and final end of human endeavor, it is also that which provides the moral content of our historical strivings and development. Chapter 4 will consider how Kant's writings on culture and history continue the theme of the interdependence of individual and community and provide a historical perspective on the concept of moral development.

4

Cultural Differentiation:
The Origins of History

The social character of moral development and the interdependence of individual and community are constant themes of Kant's writings on history. "Idea for a Universal History from a Cosmopolitan Point of View" states the case most boldly. Unfolding the implications of a teleological view of nature, Kant, in the First Thesis, maintains that "all natural capacities of a creature are destined to evolve completely to their natural end."[1]

However, mankind is uniquely characterized by a far greater dependency of the individual on the species than is the case for animals generally. Kant writes in the Second Thesis that "those natural capacities which are directed to the use of reason" develop fully only in the species, not in the individual.[2] Apparently, it is not our natural capacities per se that create this greater social dependence, but our natural capacities insofar as they are *directed to the use of reason*.

In "Kant's Historical Materialism," Allen Wood explains how this heuristic "biological" principle is transformed into a historical narrative because of the unique impact of reason on the development of the capacities of the species. He expresses the consequences of any attempt to study the human species:

> This means that when we set out to study human beings, our object of study must be collective in yet another sense: it must be historical, encompassing the processes by which people acquire new capacities, assimilate them into their life–activities, and transmit them to their descendants. Thus not only is

the human race as a biological species, essentially historical, but the study of this species must be fundamentally historical.[3]

Wood concludes that on Kant's view the nature of human beings is such that any attempt to construct a science of society on "micro foundations" is fundamentally flawed. Philosophical history, which presents the organizing teleological framework for human development, is then a necessary condition of any empirical study of the human species as a natural phenomenon.

This view of mankind's teleological destiny contains a potential paradox. The complete development or perfection inherent to the exercise of our natural capacities is frustrated by the nature of reason. Reason expands the purposes and limits of all other natural powers beyond instinct, creating potential conflicts between different natural ends. And reason does not itself work automatically. Reason requires trial and error, practice and instruction, wherein the only hope of progress is the ability to add the experience of one individual to the experience of another. Individuals with their limited life spans, taken in isolation, are incapable of this extended "rational" development. Even the genius cannot escape from the frustration of this limitation. Although the inventions and discoveries of the exceptional few have a public character, they must be preserved if their productions are to be built upon. The remedy for this otherwise debilitating limitation is culture. Culture is the medium through which one generation passes on its collective experience and practice to another generation. Although the full development of all rational capacities is described as "Nature's purpose," this natural end is at the same time the goal of mankind's collective efforts through which cultures are formed and developed and from which practical freedom emerges. In creating a finite rational creature, nature has created a social species that is, in a sense, destined to evolve its powers over time. Because of its spontaneous character, reason has created a problem and a task that only reason in its extended social–practical sense can solve. The Kantian formulation of the "teleological problem," then, is not a problem within a purely naturalist or materialist framework. Teleology arises from the needs of reason and the conflicts that this creates can only be resolved "autonomously," in terms of reason's capacity to formulate its own principles for development.

As Richard Velkley has so eloquently formulated the issue in his recent study of the teleological origins of Kant's Critical Philosophy, *Freedom and the End of Reason*: "[O]nly the common moral reason (which by its nature, in Kant's view, aims at consistency and unity) can be the highest principle for the direction of reason, nullifying the internal 'dialectic' of reason as instrumental to given natural ends."[4]

Velkley persuasively argues that the Critical Philosophy is not a rejection of teleology but a replacement of naturalist teleology with a new doctrine of the end of reason whose aim is to complete the foundation for the modern liberal project of "emancipation" from natural constraints. According to Velkley, the entire critical project is best understood as a critique of practical reason—a search for the pure or noninstrumental conditions of its employment. Only the autonomy of reason can guarantee its ultimate perfection and thereby also provide a telos for a rational species. If the development of practical reason is embedded in a historical process of cultural evolution, then critical theory is not complete without an articulation of the goal of this process. In "Idea for a Universal History" Kant identifies this goal as a cosmopolitan culture.

The "ideal of morality," Kant says "belongs to culture,"[5] and specifically to a cosmopolitan condition within which the rational capacities of the species will be perfected. Moral development is inscribed within the Kantian definition of culture. Culture then is an essential component of human moral development. But what exactly is Kant's theory of culture? In particular, if humanity is destined for a "final end" in the form of a cosmopolitan culture, why do cultures differentiate and engage in deadly conflict? What is the relationship between cultural pluralism and cosmopolitanism?

In "Conjectural Beginning of Human History" Kant turns to the question of the origin of human culture. In this essay he provides an interesting explanation of the development of cultural difference as an outgrowth of the exercise of reason and an expression of human freedom.[6] Kant's concern in this essay is not with the record of human deeds, which, he notes, is the work of the historian, but with the *origins* of human action in its natural context.

Since this is a speculative inquiry, Kant assumes general experience can be our guide "if only one presupposes that human actions were in the first beginning no better and no worse than we find them now."[7] This assumption (which, Kant explains, draws on an analogy with nature) expresses also the idea of a continuity in the character of the species that permits the reader to identify with the fictive agents of the story. It is the specific structure of human freedom that Kant wishes to trace.

Like Genesis, Kant begins his account with a single adult pair whose rational faculties have already emerged. Unlike the biblical account, Kant assumes that these faculties have been acquired by man himself. Since a complete theory of the stages of this acquisition would involve

many additional "conjectures" and is unimportant to the main purpose of the tale, Kant proceeds to explicate the critical experiment
underlying the development of human "manners and morals."

According to Kant's account, no special but lost abilities need to
be postulated to explain the difference between our original and present
condition. Once the specific structure of human freedom is imaginatively outlined, the differences in historical situations can be filled in
through the historical record. Even the activity of instinct is assumed
to be continuous with the natural ability of man's senses when properly functioning to detect appropriate objects of consumption. One
need then only assume an exercise of reason to explain the possibility
of divergence from the course originally provided by nature. Reason
need only institute a comparison between the ordinary object of the
senses and a newly presented object for this experiment to begin and
for the structure of freedom to emerge.

By instituting a comparison between the normal or instinctive
objects of sense and a novel object, reason, the faculty of formulating
and widening rule, extends "knowledge" of potential objects. If the
experiment is not contrary to what instinct directs, no harm is done.
However, incipient reason has a further peculiarity in that it can engage with the power of imagination and thereby create *artificial* objects
of desire. These objects are artificial in that instinct alone would never
have suggested them. Their character is further transformed because
imagination, by refashioning the object into an internal representation, removes the object from its immediate natural context, makes its
presence more constant, and extends its influence. This ability to extend desire beyond instinct is the first step in the development of the
power of choice, which in turn provides the possibility of the *deliberate*
deviation from natural instinct. Nature must cooperate in the sense
that our initial choices must have been compatible with our survival,
but the immediate ground of this deviation is not "nature'" but practical reason. We can see in Kant's analysis of mankind's "conjectural
beginning" the powerful influence of Rousseau's view of the unnatu-
ralness of reason's role in removing mankind from the tutelage of
nature. Although human desire is artificial in relation to nature, the
development of desire is neither arbitrary nor accidental, but is entailed by the existence of reason. While in relation to nature practical
reason introduces an element of arbitrariness into the realm of human
experience, the instrumental character of reason creates the reflective
conditions for the apprehension of the special status of humanity. The
conscious use of nature as a "means" produces the contrasting awareness of oneself as an "end." Of this pivotal choice Kant says: "The first
time he ever said to the sheep, 'nature has given you the skin you

wear for my use, not for yours' . . . that time he became aware of the way in which his nature privileged and raised him above all animals."[8]

The first effect of freedom, the conscious power of choice, is irreversible. It carries with it the mark of man as an end and foreshadows the destiny of the species, *that is, the complete development of all rational capacities.* Human history is irreversible and progressive because practical reason introduces its own teleology and principle of development. The "appearance" of the fully human being coincides with the separation of history and nature and with the introduction of a higher standard for human development than natural pleasure.

By releasing man from instinctual direction, practical reason enlarges the scope of purposive activity, but also carries with it the danger that some of these purposes will conflict. In fact, culture, the social organization of these choices, interferes with some of the most basic natural functions by continuously altering the conditions to which they have been adapted. In turn, natural impulses impede the progress of culture. Since reason is thoroughly implicated in the foundations of this conflict, mankind's final moral end must include the resolution of these conflicts. A moral culture will provide the final and complete perfection of mankind as a natural species as well as a moral one.

Kant continues his analysis of "manners and morals" by tracing the origin of distinctive views of property, social organization, and deity in the development of particular "ways of life" or cultures. Cultural difference—first, in the sense that marks mankind apart from other natural creatures, and later in the sense that separates human groups—emerges from practical reason's power of choice and ability to set arbitrary purposes. Nature provides for these initial possibilities, but it is through the human selection and shaping of these natural conditions that cultural artifacts such as property arise.

Kant's account of the origins of cultural history in "Conjectural Beginning," while on the surface but the retelling of the biblical tale of Cain and Abel, differs from that story in ways that reveal the *social roots of morality*, specifically the origins of moral evil. The actors in this tale are not individuals in the modern sense, but representatives of different "ways of life." Although occupying the same general area, one has chosen to cultivate the land and the other has chosen to raise and tend animals.

This early form of "cultural differentiation" soon leads to conflict, but unlike the biblical account, Kant does not portray primitive man as inherently jealous, malicious, or murderous. In Kant's version conflict arises out of the unforeseen and unintended consequences of equally legitimate but different uses of natural communal property (in the sense that the earth originally belongs to all). Labor-intensive agriculture, for instance, depends upon secure and permanent possession of land. Herding, however, requires large tracts of land that can remain open to the changing needs of the animals. In Kant's version of the original conflict, the herdsman's cattle unwittingly trammel the farmer's crops. The herdsman, Kant speculates, being "conscious of no wrongdoing" stands his ground while the angry farmer removes himself from this "nuisance" and establishes a separate community. Kant writes: "Until that time men had lived peacefully side by side. But here that strife had to begin which separated those of a different way of life and dispersed men all over the earth."[9]

Different "ways of life" create different needs that come into conflict. But since initially nature is rich in resource and reason is as yet immature, there is neither need nor inclination to resort to negotiation. Neither is there apparently any particular interest in violence, a major divergence from the biblical version of the original conflict. Those of different "manners" simply separate and differentiate.

Cultural differentiation, intrinsic to practical reason's development, precedes and conditions later ideological conflict. Separate development will in time lead to distinctive views of the nature of property with different conceptions of "rights" and law, different types of social organization, different views of the deity, and different languages. These linguistic and conceptual differences will, when interaction becomes unavoidable, make the negotiation of conflicting purposes more difficult for a human reason that has remained immature.[10] Immaturity will give way to moral weakness, a preference for one's own interests in disregard of the interests of others, and from this the mutual disposition to injury, injustice, and war will be born. Nonetheless, Kant maintains here that a peace that ends conflict by simply suppressing cultural differences would not be morally beneficial. For Kant the value of peace derives not from a simple self-preservation, but from its relationship to a fully developed freedom. Therefore Kant reminds us: "Only in a state of perfect culture would perpetual peace be of benefit to us, and only then would it be possible."[11]

A state of perfect culture, implying as it does the complete development of our rational capacities and powers, would presuppose the resolution of their conflicting purposes. However, an imposed peace is not a "resolution" in this sense. Reason, the source of these conflicts, must develop through its own internal capacities the critical and legislative power to integrate ends. The resolution that results from a developed reason is simultaneously the unfolding of genuine or perpetual peace.

While undoubtedly many evils arise from war, there is another difficulty growing out of cultural dependence that is also a source of misfortune for the individual. Following Rousseau, Kant maintains that there is an inevitable conflict between culture and the natural dispositions of the human species. One very basic example of this conflict is expressed in the ambiguous status of youth in a civil condition. Human beings achieve physical maturity, with the desire and capacity to reproduce, in their teenage years. However, they do not typically attain civil maturity, defined in terms of the acquisition of the skills and economics resources to support a family, until many years later. Worse yet, social inequality of access to these resources may disadvantage some in attaining their natural goals. Social dependence and social complexity are at the root of these difficulties. Like Rousseau, Kant refuses to blame nature for the evils that arise from these conflicts, for nature disposes creatures toward the good. Rather, these evils are the fault of an imperfect culture that can be rectified by human action. For Kant the perfection of culture is a purpose of nature in endowing humanity with reason. Kant credits Rousseau with at least attempting to solve the ultimate problem: "how culture was to move forward, in order to bring about such a development of the dispositions of mankind, considered as a moral species, as to end the conflict between the natural and the moral species."[12]

In a sense, nature has provided humanity with a dual vocation: one as a natural and the other as a moral species. The development of culture, which is a good for the species, generates disorder within desire and inequality between individuals, and frequently entails evils for the individual. From this perspective, nature has been unkind toward the individual, rather like a neglectful stepmother. These evils express fundamental "injustices" that pervade human culture, the removal of which would promote the highest good—the condition in which virtue, or the moral good, would be accompanied by the natural good of happiness. The development of humanity as a moral species requires the perfection of human culture. To reach the "ultimate moral end" of the species, culture must move forward "as the genuine education of man as man and citizen" in the context of a civil society.[13] Justice, then, has a natural component because it must look also to our natural good.

Insofar as we try to understand nature's purpose in relation to humanity, we must include the existence of our rational and social capacities in our concept of purposiveness. But this sense of purposiveness is no longer merely external or relative. Through the activity of practical reason, the development of our rational and social capacities becomes purposive in an internal or intentional sense. Through the development of culture, practical reason imposes a form of moral purposiveness onto the natural world.

Individuals can resolve the problems presented by cultural development only in social context. But Kant does not exempt the individual from culpability for the existence of social ills. The projection of the present onto a simpler condition presents the prospect of a new beginning. But each individual's exercise of freedom, regardless of historical place, faces the same tasks and process of development. "Conjectural Beginning" is presumably about the actions of agents from the distant past, yet Kant advises his contemporary reader to regard these initial acts as his own.

> Such an exposition teaches man that, under like circumstances, he would act exactly like his first parents, that is, abuse reason in the very first use of reason. . . . Hence he must recognize what they have done as his own act, and thus blame himself for the evils which spring from the abuse of reason.[14]

After all, the present condition of culture is not that far removed from this conjectural beginning, and Kant presumes that individuals continue to desire the fruits of culture even while they complain of its bitterness. The distinction between mere pleasure and value, which can only be generated by free action, is intrinsic to the human condition. The analysis of human beginnings is intended to remind even the thoughtless man of this truth. Kant says: "The foregoing presentation of man's original state teaches us that, because he could not be satisfied with it, man could not remain in this state, much less be inclined ever to return to it; that therefore, he must, after all, ascribe his present troublesome condition to himself and his own choice."[15]

In a manner foreshadowing Sartre's conviction of total responsibility for the condition of one's times, Kant issues a call to take responsibility for one's "troublesome condition." What began as a speculative analysis of the generic origins of human action ends as a universal practical admonition. We are asked to recognize that we do not in fact really desire simplicity and that our own choices have implicit within them the seeds of these historical conflicts. In fact, human happiness is shown to be not a simple hedonic concept. Many of our desires, originating in imagination, are artificial. They frequently involve a comparison of our condition with that of others, and thereby contain an inherently social and cultural dimension. To become worthy of happiness, we must create a form of happiness compatible with social justice. Kant's conception of human nature and its historical development through the perfection of culture allows him to presume an interdependence between the individual and the species and thereby a strong connection between a personal and a social good. This connection is possible because humanity is, I have argued, for Kant both a natural and a moral species (which is certainly not an assumption acceptable to Sartre). Kant's assertion that individuals have a "natural interest" in the development of their species in the form of an interest in their history is an important adjunct to the character of moral agency. This sense of "vocation" is intended to counter the discontent that arises from the difficulties of the task. The promotion of the highest good entails a personal obligation to contribute toward a social goal attainable only by the species. Insofar as the species has a moral destiny, the "vocation" to contribute to it can be viewed as an aspect of the individual's moral development.

Given Kant's notion of humanity's moral destiny in "Conjectural Beginning," it should not be surprising that, when he develops his theory of moral evil in the *Religion*, Kant locates the sources of moral failing within humanity itself, that is, in the *propensity to evil innate to the species.* It can now be seen that the theory of "radical evil" outlined in chapter 3 is complementary to his perspective on cultural/historical development. This propensity, arising from a fundamental choice subordinating the moral incentive to the generalized incentive of self-love, corrupts the predisposition to humanity, the ground of all of our social inclinations. Within the predisposition to humanity, nature apparently has created quite a brew. This predisposition is associated with a general self-love that is motivated by a rational comparison of conditions. The original desires for equality and esteem are natural adjuncts to our moral personality, and the idea of "rivalry"—which, Kant notes, does not exclude mutual love—is a useful "spur to culture."

But when these natural desires are disturbed by the apparent attempts of others to gain superiority, vices arise. Kant tells us that the resulting "vices which are grafted upon this inclination might be their [sic] termed vices of *culture*."[16] In this context of social competition, the generalized preference for self-love appears as a kind of social insurance policy. But, despite the fact that this is, in essence, the "human condition," morality continues to demand that we strive toward the overcoming of this "ethical state of nature." Kant apparently did not hold individual responsibility to be exclusive of faults pertaining to our humanity, and he clearly held individuals to be responsible for the promotion of moral goals that are ultimately social in their significance.

"Conjectural Beginning of Human History" leaves us with a complex view of human development that places the internal perfection of culture and the adjudication of cultural differences at the constantly moving center of "moral progress." Perpetual peace, we recall, requires a perfect culture, and a perfect culture will include the full development of all mankind's capacities—that is, it will manifest the fullest possible differentiation of "culture." The adjudication of these differences will require the development of an international community, a cosmopolitan culture, to articulate an international code of justice. Only an international code of justice will enable the species to solve the problem of peace in a manner consistent with the human right to cultural autonomy. Cultural autonomy is a morally significant type of autonomy, because cultural differentiation is an outcome of reason's own spontaneity. Culture is the first fruit of freedom. But it is also socially constructed and the product of human conflict. Kant's theory of culture in "Conjectural Beginning" leads back naturally to the philosophy of history articulated in "Idea," where the problem of a perfect civil society and the problem of a just international order are connected. The articulation of a historical telos or goal for human cultural development is required to provide a guide for the maximum integration and resolution of these conflicting claims.

5

Purposiveness and
Political Progress

In the last chapter I argued that, given the nature of reason, human development is inherently a social task. I concluded that cultural elaboration and differentiation are implicit in the spontaneous character of reason and are therefore an aspect of human autonomy. The resulting pluralism presents more than just the problem of peaceable coexistence. Kant's view of human development demands that all of the rational capacities of humanity be fully developed in a just and equitable manner. For this to occur, all cultures would have to eventually participate in some form of global development. Reason is thus invested in a cosmopolitan teleological program. In the last chapter we saw how cultural development results in intrasocial conflicts, and intercultural interactions can produce additional levels of inequality and injustice. Thus, the problem of peace must be solved within the framework of a global justice.[1]

The organization of cultures into states is a necessary moment in bringing lawful order to the development of natural differences and in rectifying the inequalities that emerge from this process. The emergence of multiple independent nations brings to the foreground the issue of international relations and the problem of the peaceful interaction between autonomous states whose views of justice may also conflict. An international code of justice is a prerequisite for the full development of our moral duties because these duties, unlike those arising from positive law, include the whole of mankind. Since no one can fulfill these duties properly until such time as the race has solved the problem of peace in a manner consistent with cultural autonomy, the individual cannot attain a better empirical character than the character of his or her society.[2] In particular, my ability to act in a just manner will be constrained by the given system of rights.[3] The systems of rights that characterize a particular community of nations are in turn all provisional until a system of international law is recognized as binding. If the conflict of national rights is without remedy, perpetual peace, a condition of the highest good, would become an empty ideal. This is turn would mean that mankind cannot be conceived as a moral species, and all moral laws would be reduced to illusion.

Given that justice is a global developmental project, affected by multiple levels of human difference, how can we tell when the policies of our particular society are making a "positive" contribution? Despite the natural interest that we have in the history of the species, the sheer complexity of a merely empirical history creates an ever more serious burden of interpretation. However, Kant maintains that the tendency to regard human action as futile is not a moral option, for it would deprive humanity of rational value. Historical judgment must provide the point of view, rooted in our moral interests, that organizes this complexity. Kant maintains that later generations "will naturally value the history of earlier time . . . only from the point of view of what interests them, i.e., in answer to the question of what the various nations and governments have contributed to the goal of world citizenship" [4]

Judgment therefore requires orientation. Just as the body, according to Kant, serves to orient the physical self in phenomenal space, judgment must serve as the orienting mechanism in the complex multicultural space of the historical realm. Guided by our moral interests, reflective judgment must identify the "progressive" elements in the collection of human deeds that can be further shaped and constructed as historical "signs" of development. By identifying the conditions that promote moral goals, individuals can design their own actions to contribute further to these ends.

What type of knowledge is it that demonstrates the "purposiveness" of phenomena in relation to moral goals? Is the political realm, part of the realm of "appearances," subject to this type of knowledge? Is the "moral interest" in these goals sufficient to orient the judging subject who has her or his own subjective interests? The problem of identifying political progress is deepened by Kant's conception that the human will is "handicapped" by a universal propensity to evil. Historical progress, however it is measured, must be possible within the constraints of a morally imperfect will. Does moral imperfection corrupt our judgment? Can an immoral population engage in disinterested judgment? How can moral progress ever be attributed to an imperfectly moral species?

Fortunately, Kant's conception of evil is such that an "interest" in moral ends is never fully relinquished even on the part of the wicked. The recognition of moral purposiveness is not dependent upon morally good character. This parallels the situation of the individual in relation to the moral law. The morally deficient individual does not lose the capacity for moral judgment. An interest in the moral law is retained even in his or her consciousness of "deviation" from the moral law. In fact, this "interest" is important for Kant's theory of accountability in that the criminal must be capable of spontaneously recognizing the validity of the moral law for punishment to be justified.

Disinterested political judgment, then, provides an analogue of this individual moral judgment. Such judgments discern the ideal tendency of a series of acts even while recognizing that the particular event is imperfectly constituted. Despite the continuous presence of evil, through our incorruptible capacity to discern the ideal, disinterested political judgment grounds the hope that political reforms will contribute to the realization of moral goals. Can such an interest that is specifically focused on humanity's moral goals be empirically demonstrated? And what does this imply concerning individual moral duty?

Historical progress implies that humanity, and not just individual human beings, has purposes that can be identified. Having identified these, there must be a link between these moral–political goals of humanity and the moral goals of individuals. Without this link the problem of the historical use of individuals as "mere means" to the ends of future generations renders Kant's general ethical system incoherent. Individuals have an obligation to overcome evil and to perfect their own dispositions. The ethical commonwealth as a condition for the overcoming of evil is that link. If individuals have an obligation to promote a universal social good as a condition of their own moral perfection, then the tension between individual dignity and historical goals is superseded. And if individuals have a moral interest in the interests of humanity, then it must be possible to judge when particular actions and events contribute toward this goal, for we cannot have a duty that we cannot know how to fulfill.

Judgment must have a dimension that can apprehend the moral purposiveness of those human achievements which transcend individual intention, which are social in their significance and are culturally sustained and transmitted. These achievements are the patterns and rituals, the social organization of activity, that we call "cultural" objects, some of which also fall under the rubric of law in the narrow sense of legal institutions. Although the purposiveness of culture is initially treated by Kant as a natural telos, it is from the beginning a subjective reflective concept. The complete articulation of culture in terms of the full development of the rational powers of the species places this natural telos under the faculty of freedom and hence transfers it into the realm of practical principles.

Reason deals with universal goals; judgment must specify how the universal can be approached by apprehending what is of universal significance in the particular. Since purposiveness partakes of the rational, judgments of the purposiveness of social–cultural activities are not a merely local matter whose relevance is limited to primary participants. The purposiveness of social–cultural activities is accessible and significant to the nonparticipant observer as well. That some generic level of purposiveness is a constitutive element of human cultures is a presupposition of cultural anthropology. If something of general human significance can be appreciated through the study of specific cultures, then there must also be some form of relative or external purposiveness that they express, some system of intersubjective significance to which they belong.

Does such a general system of intersubjective meanings also display a progressive character? A tendency of change toward a discernible ideal? Since the matter of such an investigation is the human subject, the projection of such ideals would seem to lead to a kind of disclosure or unfolding of what is meant by "humanity" as a moral species.

In "An Old Question: Is the Human Race Constantly Progressing?" Kant addresses the issue of historical progress in a manner that takes the organization of peoples into states as the critical standpoint for analysis. The choice of standpoint is doubly important because lawfulness is not a product of direct empirical observation and individual free actions introduce an element of randomness that make "human affairs" seem senseless. Only reason, Kant tells us, can select the proper standpoint. Only reason grasps "totalities" and through these wholes guides the quest for empirical regularities. Moreover, with respect to human history, human beings can assume a certain insight into social constructions, such as the state, that are founded upon rational practical principles. Thus if one desires to know something of "future" human history, if the question is one of moral progress, then one must, according to Kant, adopt the standpoint of "the totality of men united socially on earth and apportioned into peoples."[5]

This standpoint of the totality of social unions reveals a universal tendency of nations to adjust their organizations toward a specific historical goal, a peaceful federation of republics. Empirical data confirms that wars and revolutions affect the commercial interests and internal development of all nations, leading statesmen to form alliances and to offer mediation in the resolution of conflicts. These alliances in turn provide the nucleus for new and stronger political formations, enabling the evolution of principles of international law and the emergence of a world order. Although in "Idea" Kant had maintained that most of human history proceeds without a "plan," the intentions of statesmen in promoting this federation are not the primary object of historical judgments concerning political progress. Having assumed a cosmopolitan standpoint, Kant's concern is to establish the relationship between reflective judgment and certain types of events. Historical progress is revealed in the correspondence between judgment and event.

What kind of judgment and what kind of event count for discerning historical progress? In "An Old Question," Kant maintains that even in the apparently chaotic events of politics, of revolution and war, an interest in the moral ends of humanity is evidenced by the "moral enthusiasm" and "disinterested sympathy" that ordinary people display at the sight of struggles to institute republican constitutions. With nothing personal to gain and often at some risk, such sympathy displays a certain solidarity with moral objectives. Genuine enthusiasm, Kant tells us, is motivated only by what is "Ideal" and is incompatible with self-interest. Such a response is important for anthropology, because it reveals a moral quality within humanity. Kant claims that these judgments reveal a genuine "moral predisposition" that, because it is a fundamental attribute of the human subject, is sufficient to underwrite a moral progress. This underwriting appears in the claim that the objectives of republicanism and peace are

> too much interwoven with the interest of humanity . . . not to be recalled on any favorable occasion. . . . For such a phenomenon in human history is not to be forgotten, for it has revealed a tendency and faculty in human nature for improvement.[6]

What Kant seems to be saying here is that however imperfectly these objectives are achieved, they are spontaneously recognized by even the imperfect moral subject as the requirements of justice and therefore as contributions toward humanity's moral goal. The institutional innovations underlying republican constitutions are certified as "progressive" by such judgments. Furthermore, circumstances permitting, such external innovations excite a will to participate in the further promotion of human progress. Thus, the ability to be the "cause of our own improvement" is not limited to agents of revolution, but trickles down indefinitely in the form of inspiration to all who witness the events—presumably, even to those later generations who receive this information at second hand from the professional historian. History is, on this account, a form of "witnessing" and so is of primary importance to the collective appropriation of humanity's moral character.

The periodic expression of humanity's moral predisposition in the
form of moral enthusiasm is not a cause in the ordinary empirical
sense. It is not the "cause" of the historical event as a phenomenon.
But then neither is it an empirical "effect." Causal explanations of particular events do not depend upon these judgments, nor do they include them. But historical "understanding" in its full sense requires
reflective judgment, because to grasp the significance of a complex
series of events requires the recognition of some sorts of patterns and
the determination of some kind of whole. What is judged is not a
particular act, but a character or quality of a series of actions that
makes these particulars parts of a larger whole. Some collective actions "fit" the pattern of the moral goal, just as some of the actions of
individuals fit the pattern of certain maxims and some objects fit the
form of the beautiful.

Kant refers to the event that is the occasion for the expression of
moral enthusiasm as a "historical sign," noting that the prediction of
future efforts is not based on the specific actions of individuals (which
would involve an interminable calculation) but rather on the "tendency of the human race viewed in its entirety . . . as divided into
nations and states."[7] This tendency or character of the whole allows us
to see certain phenomena as representations or "signs" of certain goals.
The enthusiasm with which the struggles of the French revolutionaries
to institute a republic was met is a sign that republicanism is a moral
goal of actual human history. It is not the phenomenon taken in isolation nor emotion per se that allows this prognosis. It is the interplay of
event and response that provides the basis of "prophetic history." Kant
is thus emboldened to call such sympathetic judgments evidence of a
moral cause operating within history, yet "undetermined with respect
to time." Always present and sometimes apparent, such a "cause" is
really the affirmation of the human capacity for moral self-development. Furthermore, such a response is not just a predictor of what can
be anticipated for the future; it is also, according to Kant, a basis for
the projection onto the past of the permanent tendency of the human
species.[8] Such judgments do not change the nature of past events.
They do not cancel existing empirical descriptions. Rather, such judgments resignify or reconstitute the meaning of the past in relation to
future goals. To resignify the past is the constant purpose of historical
judgment. Kant confidently concludes:

> The human race has always been in progress. . . . To him who
> does not consider what happens in some one nation but also

has regard to the whole scope of peoples on earth who will gradually come to participate, this reveals . . .[9]

In projecting the final goal of history, Kant's overall reasoning seems to be that beings who make their own history (cultural beings) and also assert claims of justice (political beings) are capable of moral development. The form of this development is predictable in advance since only a federative union of republics can establish cultural self-determination as a universal human right.

Is this "Old Question" a piece of optimistic reverie at odds with the rest of Kant's writings? A kind of regression into wishful thinking? Is this casting of humanity as a moral subject unrelated to other aspects of Kant's moral system, which are frequently cast in individualistic terms? It is helpful to recall that Kant's *Religion* begins with an anthropological analysis. Part 1 contains an extended analysis of human predispositions. These predispositions constitute the Kantian theory of human nature and are important for a proper understanding of practical freedom. The predisposition to the good, which takes three forms, appears in Kant's *Religion* as an essential element in his definition of a human being. These predispositions, all of which are related to *Willkur*, the faculty of desire, are said to be "original" in that they are "bound up with the possibility of human nature."[10] Human nature so understood connects the faculty of practical freedom to the exercise and development of predispositions to the good (moral capacities). Thus morality becomes the highest expression or articulation of human purposiveness.

While all three predispositions are inherently good, the first two, animality and humanity can be used contrary to their ends. As we saw in Chapter 4, the very development of practical freedom entailed a certain extension and eventual corruption of our original natural ends. Only the third, the predisposition to personality, *cannot be grafted onto anything evil*. It can at most be subordinated to other ends. However, possession of the predisposition to personality is not in itself good character. Good character would require the free adoption of the moral law as a sufficient incentive of the will. Kant's analysis in the *Religion* reveals the human will as a complex structure wherein the incentive of self-love competes for supremacy with the moral law. Unlike a holy will, the moral law is not the *sole incentive* for the human will.

Given the depths of the incentive of self-love, Kant maintains that there must be something already present in the subjective constitution of humanity that predisposes us toward the adoption of the moral law. Otherwise, the free adoption of morality would be arbitrary. And clearly for Kant there is nothing arbitrary about morality. There must

therefore be something in the *nature* of the creature that makes morality both possible and fulfilling. This predisposition to personality that
disposes us toward the adoption of the moral law is both original and,
like the others, inalienable. Humanity is then neither the blank slate of
empiricism nor fully plastic. Human nature is defined in terms of moral
capacities (of which sympathy is an expression) that must be developed through the exercise of freedom. It is the anthropological sub-
strate of these moral capacities, present in the species being, which
makes moral progress possible and provides a watershed against an
unending moral retrogression. Thus the vision of humanity as a moral
subject found in the writings on history is confirmed and supported
by the anthropology of Kant's *Religion*. While at any point in time, due
to the continuing influence of the propensity to evil, the character of
the human race may be "evil," the predisposition of humanity cannot
be so.[11] Humanity as a species is neither a race of devils nor of angels.

As I argued in chapter 3, Kant maintains in the *Religion* that due to
the propensity to evil the "character" of the species is "evil." The propensity to evil is not, however, an essential element of a human being.
It is not part of the definition of being human, nor part of the concept
of man. Michalson says of Kant's intention: "His effort, for example, to
distinguish the predisposition to good from the propensity to evil is
partly an effort to avoid associating moral evil with the sheer fact that
we are sensuous beings, but to associate it instead with a free response
to our sensuousness."[12]

Nothing in nature per se is evil. This gives the predisposition to
personality a kind of edge up on the propensity to evil, because this
propensity cannot ultimately corrupt the basic orientation of the species toward the good. Nonetheless, this propensity is said to be innate
in a special sense. Because this propensity is an expression of a basic
act of freedom, it cannot be located as a specific event in time.[13] The
propensity to evil, then, must be due to the corruption of something
basic to the creature's constitution. This cannot be, as we have seen,
the predisposition to personality. If this were corruptible, human beings could never regain the moral incentive and would lose all accountability for their actions. The predisposition to humanity is the best
candidate, because this predisposition works with the comparative
form of practical reason (not the mechanical form characteristic of
animality) arising in connection with our social condition.[14] And as we
have seen, practical freedom arises from the development of practical
reason in a social context. Thus, through the predisposition to humanity, the propensity to evil is connected with the faculty of freedom
and our social condition from the very beginning.

Since the origins of human history are coeval with the origins of culture, there is no specific point of time from which to mark the appearance of this propensity. It is timeless in the same way that the origins of history and culture are timeless. As Kant maintains in "Conjectural Beginning of Human History," "The history of nature therefore begins with good, for it is the work of God, while the history of freedom begins with wickedness, for it is the work of man."[15]

Nonetheless, it is a duty to overcome this propensity. Although the individual must strive to overcome this propensity in her or his own disposition, this duty is not only a duty of the individual. It is also a duty of the species, because the only means adequate to the elimination of the propensity to evil, the ethical commonwealth, is a social goal. This means that even well-disposed individuals, acting alone, cannot eliminate the power of the propensity to evil inhering in the social interactions of human beings. Even the morally well-disposed individual must adopt as an end the promotion of an ethical community. An ethical community is therefore more than an aggregate of private intentions. An ethical community is a public association whose members commit themselves to public principles of virtue.[16] The intelligible kingdom of ends articulated in the Groundwork must, in light of the propensity to evil, take a social and historical form: that of the ethical commonwealth.

Because the predisposition to the good can neither be corrupted nor eliminated as long as we remain human, it endures as a universal and timeless cause of moral development. While we cannot know or calculate its strength to affect the evil that has been brought into the human condition, through our reflections on history we can discover the "profit" or consequences that result from our efforts to reform existing social conditions. We can measure the increase in discipline, lawful conduct, and good deeds, which we can legitimately anticipate will transform the character of our social interactions. And when the character of our social interactions has been transformed, we can rightfully expect that the power of the propensity to evil will be lessened.[17]

Since the species doesn't "act," we can only know the presence of this predisposition as a universal cause under particular circumstances, as revealed in our disinterested judgments concerning public events. Our capacity to sympathize reveals this aspect of ideal humanity as present and enduring, as unaffected by the evil still operative in the human condition. Kant thus invests tremendous power and significance in the realm of disinterested judgment from which public dialogue takes its root. These judgments orient our feeling, thinking, and action toward the ideal. We can only asses the character and progress of the species against this background.

By its nature, the idea of moral progress entails the possibility of a predictive or "prophetic" moral history. But according to Kant, it does not depend upon a supernatural form of knowledge. The subject matter of a universal moral history is human action, and human subjects, authoring these actions, can know something of the character of what they themselves produce.

If human actions do not appear to display a lawful character, Kant speculates it may be due to the perspective from which they are viewed. The motions of the planets, he notes, appear erratic from the perspective of the earth, but assume a regular order from the standpoint of the sun. Since we do not literally stand on the sun, this change of perspective requires an "act of reason." It requires an ability to spontaneously adopt a perspective on the whole of which we are a part.[18] If progress is an attribute of the human race, then our perspective will have to include the totality of all peoples; it will have to be a universal history.

We have seen that Kant stipulates further that a universal history requires the perspective of this totality as divided into nations and states. This is the Rosetta stone necessary to read the tendency of a universal moral history. Why is this particular mode of organization necessary in order to anticipate the character of future human actions?

Kant's theory of the state serves several important functions. It protects historically generated forms of autonomy by preserving social organization and culture. The state also serves a moral function insofar as it secures the maximal expression and development of external freedom. Finally, the state is a "mode of practical knowledge," because as one element within a complex system of international law it is a marker and vehicle for our apprehension of moral progress.

While the *Groundwork* provided the formulation of the moral law, Kant's theory of moral freedom, the application of practical principles to the realm of outer freedom, is developed in his *Metaphysical Elements of Justice*. According to Kant we can know something concerning the character of outer freedom insofar as external freedom is ordered in accordance with principles of justice. We can know when an action is right because the conformity of the action to principles of justice constitutes the rightness of the action. We do not need insight into the motive of the action in order to determine its character as rightful. This allows for the external enforcement of duties of justice and so provides a foothold in the phenomenal world for moral development. While justice is a necessary condition of moral freedom, it does not stipulate the ends that are our duties. For this, principles of virtue are necessary, and a far more complex process of assessment, articulated within an ethical community, is required to situate these ends within the order established by justice.

The principles that shape the political realm are a form of practical knowledge. Practical knowledge is complete in its own realm and it is not subordinate to our knowledge of the sensible world. But justice, although complete and determinate in its own character, is no simple matter to implement in the historical world. In the *Metaphysical Elements of Justice*, Kant outlines three forms of law: national, international, and world law. He then tells us that unless each is circumscribed by its own principles and until the *tripartite order is complete*, no part will be secured. "Consequently, if just one of these possible forms of juridical condition lacks a principle circumscribing external freedom through laws, then the structure of all the others will unavoidably be undermined and must finally collapse."[19]

Justice depends upon a world international order, organized into republics and committed to peace. Nations and states are the determinate elements of this organization which must achieve the form of a world federation organized under international law. Justice, then, is something we can know as a determinate framework; but it is a framework that, from a reflective point of view, is not yet fully instantiated in the world. Moral development on this analysis has barely begun, because the conditions of justice have yet to be completed. Hence, the question *Are we making any progress?* is an intrinsic part of this reflective cognitive framework. A unique kind of knowing, knowledge that can identify the current situation in relation to the ideal, is required by the possibility of moral progress. Thus, Makkreel maintains that authentic interpretation of history requires the use of the imagination to mediate between the actual past event and a future goal, neither of which are directly intuitable. He concludes that "A divinatory history that anticipates progress toward a reflectively conceived telos must rely on the imagination to recognize the sign of a universal moral tendency in a particular factual event."[20]

Those who would offer public judgment on the moral value of social reforms must be informed both by their historical situation and its relation to a moral ideal. The moral statesman will need to foresee how his community can be positioned within an international and cosmopolitan framework.

It is important to keep in mind that the basis for the prediction of moral progress, which must express the tendency of the whole of humanity, is not to be found in the actions of individual human beings. Tendencies inferred from a mere aggregate of individual "free" actions provide a very uncertain basis for prediction. Kant looks instead to a basis within human nature, a disposition or capacity to be the cause of our own improvement. Such a disposition would not be an ordinary object of experience. Its existence would have to be inferred from some event that allows its mode of operation to be exhibited. The event Kant chooses for analysis is the French Revolution, which radically transformed the French nation state. Evidence of this disposition, Kant maintains, is provided not by the actions or deeds of the revolutionaries (which nonetheless provide the occasion), but by the response that these actions produce in the *judgments of the public at large.*

Public judgments on the course of significant political events disclose the disposition of humanity. Public debate on issues of justice—open sympathy for and advocacy of the principles of the French Revolution—were for Kant the mark of human improvement. Actions may provide the occasion for these judgments, but actions have a way of fading back into the empirical flux, whereas a transformation in the *mode of thinking* about justice marks a permanent stage in human moral progress. Public judgments express the character of humanity.

The type of judgment that Kant has identified as evidence of moral progress (he even goes so far as to say that it is moral progress) is a form of reflective judgment. It is not regulative judgment, for it is not guiding practice. And it is not a form of determinative judgment, as are the principles of justice per se. Reflective judgment is akin to aesthetic judgment in its disinterested character, but its object is not a beautiful thing. The object of reflective judgment is a historical event viewed as a purposive expression of moral progress. Like aesthetic judgment, reflective judgment is normative, claiming a subjective universality that we can expect other human subjects to share. Like aesthetic judgment, reflective judgment is grounded in a form of nonpathological feeling, namely, sympathy. The sympathy expressed in reflective judgment is a capacity to share in enduring human interests.[21] If the beautiful is an enduring human interest, so too is the interest in justice and moral progress. This enduring interest makes possible a historical community that is aroused to communication through sympathetic responses to the actual strivings of agents who may be culturally or temporally situated differently than the observer. It is the normative character of these human interests that makes intersubjective judgments concerning the meaning of historical events possible.

Rudolf Makkreel notes the crucial role that reflective judgment plays in making intersubjective judgments possible. Such judgments, according to Makkreel, articulate the Kantian notion of a *sensus communis*. He argues that "The *sensus communis* uses reflective judgment to abstract from the private empirical aspects of our subjective representations in order to generate what might be called a communal or intersubjective perspective."[22]

As noted earlier, the concept of "orientation" plays an important role in Makkreel's analysis of the work of judgment. Judgment's reflective orientation in regard to purposiveness can be either aesthetic or teleological. According to Makkreel, in the former mode judgment orients itself on the basis of the feeling of life (harmony); in the latter mode, judgment orients on the basis of the *sensus communis*, resulting in interpretations of culture and politics. By linking reflective judgment and the *sensus communis*, Makkreel has argued for a transcendental grounding of hermeneutics, one which allows us to ascertain the relevance of particular traditions to ultimate questions of truth. This, Makkreel argues, opens up "the reflective horizon of communal meaning," without which particular traditions would remain closed within themselves. The potential for a deep understanding of other traditions depends upon imaginative possibilities, intermediary positions occupied by neither the self nor others, that enlarge one's own thought. Cross-cultural and historical translation and interpretation derive from the possibility of "deep understanding" founded upon the *sensus communis*. Reflective judgment thus enables both cultural interpretation and political critique, and makes possible the human sciences, including an authentic rendering of history.[23]

Hannah Arendt's *Lectures on Kant's Political Philosophy* has been influential in calling attention to the significance of Kant's theory of judgment for the political realm.[24] But because she is also a serious critic of Kant's theory of historical progress, it is important to analyze her view concerning the relationship between judgment and the political world. In her lectures, she maintains that although Kant did not produce a singular systematic work on the nature of the political, the faculty of judgment is the cornerstone of an implicit but unwritten political philosophy. While Kant's philosophy of law and theory of the state (which Arendt curiously regards as a minor part of the political) are derived from pure practical reason, the historical reflections that bring the world of appearances into conformity with the ideals of reason are the work of the faculty of judgment. It is in the public realm of appearances that Arendt finds the essence of the political. There is important overlap between Kant and Arendt concerning the relationship of judgment to the political realm as well as important differences that it is instructive to analyze for the purpose of revealing the relationship between moral and political development. While Arendt's appreciation for the role of judgment in constituting political phenomena allows us to extend our interpretation of moral development, she transfers much of the function of ethical theory to judgment, ultimately breaking from Kant's critical standpoint altogether.

One of the key differences between Kant and Arendt stems from her conception of the uneasy tension between the idea of progress and the ideal of human dignity. As we have noted, Kantian ethical theory appears to entail both notions, and their relationship is crucial to the coherence of Kant's philosophy. Progress is imposed upon the historical process by the idea of a highest social good that will ultimately nullify evil, while individual human dignity grounds the very principles of Kantian ethical theory. Thus the question arises, can the idea of progress coexist with the respect for the particularity of individual human beings that their dignity demands? For Arendt the idea of progress threatens the inherent dignity of human beings. She writes:

> Infinite Progress is the law of the human species; at the same time, man's dignity demands that he be seen (every single one of us) in his particularity, and as such, be seen—but without comparison and independent of time—as reflecting mankind in general. In other words, the very idea of progress–if it is more than a change in circumstances and an improvement of the world–contradicts Kant's notion of man's dignity. It is against human dignity to believe in progress.[25]

Because progress effaces the particular, judgment for Arendt must affect the reconciliation between good and evil without recourse to indefinite future ideals. This marks a significant difference between her thought and that of Kant's. However, the notion that the significance of the political arises from judgment is an important point of agreement.

Arendt understands the political as the public sphere of "appearances" relating to how the world—the world of human deeds—will appear to man, how these deeds will be appraised, and what they will come to mean. The very existence of a political realm as a public realm of meanings, requires that these deeds be judged. Like Kant, Arendt maintains that human deeds are particular actions and are therefore not appraised by the faculty of thinking, which deals with universals. Like particular objects of the senses, which must be schematized to become the shared objects of experience, particular human deeds, according to Arendt, are given a general or universal meaning as exemplars. However, she claims that to see these exemplars as simply instances of a universal idea, such as progress, is to destroy their particularity and to rob humanity of its dignity. In her estimation, exemplars are elements of stories that must have their own beginning and end and must not become part of an indefinite tale. Insofar as exemplars are derived from the experiences of particular communities, they are sharable within those communities. Are we then to conclude that such stories do not have meaning outside the communities in which they originate?

Arendt agrees with Kant concerning the a priori character of the principles underlying judgment, for she assumes that the meanings inherent in the actions of historical heroes are available to some degree to nonparticipants, but it is unclear how deeply these principles reach in grounding the ideal of humanity. A universal history, which Arendt would regard as virtually meaningless, would have to include cross-cultural stories from all historical periods. Can the Kantian notion of a universal humanity carry the weight of cross-cultural and historical translations of these stories? Is there an a priori limit on the extension of a communicative community?

Arendt claims that judgment makes freedom bearable, particularly the endless rebeginnings and encounters with evil to which we must become "reconciled." Without the notion of moral progress, historical judgment must regard evil as at best a recurrent phenomena. Arendt cites with approval Cato's statement that the victorious cause pleases the gods, but the defeated cause pleases Cato.[26] Cato's example illustrates the role of judgment in preserving the particular without recourse to any universal good. It demonstrates that even though our personal good does not triumph, through our free judgment we can resist evil and take pleasure even in the defeated cause. Kant, on the other hand, resisted the Stoic identification of virtue with the complete good. His notion of progress was intended to redeem the defeated cause not just for the individual but for the indefinite human community.

Despite similarities in the public character of the political for both Arendt and Kant, important differences for their respective understanding of history arise in terms of how the moral good is defined. Arendt maintains that we cannot define the absolute or highest good without resorting to metaphysics, which she claims is made a defunct activity by the very nature of critical reason. Kant's critical revolution was a destruction of the traditional notion of metaphysics as knowledge of a world beyond experience. But critical reason was also intended to result in a new foundation for ethical and political knowledge, for the rights and obligations of human beings in this world. Reason could justify a priori principles that the faculty of judgment would apply to the phenomenal world. But in making judgment the basis of freedom and making judgment bear the weight of the reconciliation of good and evil, Arendt appears to have disconnected freedom from its anchor in ethical theory. Can human dignity really be maintained in this manner? For Arendt, the individual historian is to be the ultimate judge of human meaning. A universal history, even if it were conceivable, she argues, would rob history of its human meaning. The question between Arendt and Kant is, can history provide this reconciliation and dignity without some basis in an ethical teleology connecting reason, judgment, and the world of appearances? Can particular histories stand alone?

Does a highest moral good rob history of its "human" meaning? Kant's view of public political judgment is grounded in his moral anthropology and thus ultimately in his ethical theory. Without this anthropology with its cultural implications, Kant's ethical principles would have little social content and no explicit teleological dimension. The highest good, then, is not ultimately a metaphysical entity but a universal social goal, an ideal for historical development. This ethical teleology gives practical freedom an inherently moral dimension and structure. Whether it thereby robs humanity of its dignity depends upon whether a universal history can provide individuals with a sense of identity that sustains their particularity in relation to the universal good. Judgment—and, in particular, intersubjective public judgments—plays an important role in the historical process for Kant. Arendt's view of the role of judgment in determining the meaning of human deeds does much to uncover this important aspect of Kant's political thought and the relationship of the political to the historical process. However, linking judgment to historical progress need not render individuals a mere means to an end external to themselves. This will depend upon how particular histories are connected to a universal history. Through judgment, historically situated people must still construct the meanings implicit in the deeds that will constitute their particular histories. But these "histories" can be translated, shared, and transmitted. We have already noted how Makkreel's inclusion of interpretation in the role of reflective judgment allows for a reconciliation of foundational and hermeneutic approaches to history. Adopting the standpoint of a universal history allows for the incorporation of these particular histories.

I would contend that Kant's philosophy of history is not antithetical to his view of human dignity, insofar as the moral goals of this process can themselves be provided with historical content by human participants. In this process public judgment is our guide, while ethical principles, particularly those of human right, are our foundation. Without a foundation in ethical principles, political life cannot be linked to moral progress.

The Kantian thesis that political evolution can be regarded as a form of moral development remains nonetheless controversial. And it is not only those who like Arendt reject the idea of progress outright that find this notion objectionable. Many commentators regard the idea of moral progress as inherently contradictory and have noted that Kant himself is not always consistent in his formulations of the significance of political development.

Paul Stern believes that it is questionable to treat historical events as representing the disposition of the species, since the history of the species in not the same kind of unity as the life of a person.[27] While clearly the unity required by the idea of the moral progress of the species is not the "same kind of unity" as the unity of the person, Stern and others overlook the deep connection between the individual and the species provided by Kant's anthropology. This connection is exhibited in his concept of the moral predisposition that is present in each human person providing for the possibility of an enduring moral project. Such an enduring moral project can provide the basis of continuous sympathy and identification with events that express human moral interests across times and cultures.[28] Even Stern modifies his stance on moral progress somewhat in his admission that historical-moral development may be admissible if political progress is viewed as occurring consequent to many "moral revolutions" on the part of individual agents. This is a view also expressed by Harry Van der Linden in his notion of a "feedback cycle" in which political reforms remove obstacles to the moral development of individuals, and the moral commitments of these individuals to further political reform guide the process to a new level.[29] If one connects these insights with my thesis that individual moral revolution is intrinsically connected to the adoption of the highest good, which is a collective and social good, as one's own end, then this "means/ends" relationship is superseded. The principles of social–political evolution are not external to moral development but are internalized in the goals and judgments of the moral agent.[30]

It is, of course, not possible to identify the moral components of historical development with the certainty of the physical sciences. But to deny the possibility of moral progress in principle would be uncritically "dogmatic." To deny that moral progress is possible disconnects the logic of moral action from the logic of moral hope and frustrates the purposes for which the Critical Philosophy was instituted.

In the very beginning of his Critical Philosophy, Kant maintained that it was reason's task to address three great questions: what may I know, what must I do, and what may I hope? The structure of these questions is not arbitrary. They define reason's relation to the world and ultimately reveal the unity of reason itself. While issues of hope have been relegated to rational faith, which is by definition outside the realm of knowledge, mediating between the questions of what I must do and what I may hope is the question of *what I can anticipate* as the result of right action. This question captures the purposive character of human action linking knowledge and hope. It calls for a logic or theory of historical action. Many commentators treat empirical propositions as exhaustive of the class of theoretical statements, leaving the realm of practice outside the domain of theory. This, however, is much too simple an account of what we can theorize about. According to Kant's *Logic*, theoretical propositions can take either a being or an action as their subject. This suggests that there can be a theory of action that results in judgments about *the historical world as it ought to be*.[31] Speculative propositions concerned with what is given through sensible intuition are a subset of theoretical propositions and are not exhaustive of this class. A purely speculative account of human events in history would be limited to appearances and the "lawful" connections between them. Even these connections will be generally "statistical" and lack the necessity of a physical science.[32] But actions, to the extent that they are considered as "effects of freedom," cannot be judged by speculative principles grounded in experience alone. In addition to a speculative account of history, reason requires a practical–theoretical account of human actions as "effects of freedom" determinable by moral principles. Public principles of law and the social institutions and practices articulated in terms of practical concepts, such as rights and justice, can be viewed as the expression of a form of collective moral progress that we can only judge in terms of practical–theoretical propositions. Since practical reason is causal only through concepts, we can project moral ends only by bringing into conception those types of action which reflective judgment identifies as having a purposive relation to outcomes. In this way we come to anticipate the results of our actions. Practical reason cannot complete its cognitive function without representing the world as purposive. Reflective judgment, we have noted, can literally re-cognize the phenomena of human action, assigning moral significance to a series of appearances in relation to a moral goal. In this way particular events acquire normative significance, and some parts of the world appear as they ought to be. This re-presenting function of reflective judgment is an essential element of practical knowledge, mediating between the phenomenal and moral character of human action. Judgment thereby provides the basis for certain theoretical propositions concerning human history.

In his introduction to "Theory and Practice," Kant discusses the importance of judgment in the application of theory to practice in the natural sciences. Judgment leads to the generation of rules to facilitate application and thereby completes theory and protects it from criticism. Judgment in this context validates theory. Moral theory according to

Kant is on even firmer ground than natural science, because the concept of duty directly determines the value of the practice that follows
from it. Only the impossibility of the attainment of a goal would invalidate it as an end of moral theory. Kant distinguishes in this essay
three areas of moral theory. The first deals with the welfare of the
individual, the second with the welfare of the state, and the third with
the welfare of the human race as a whole. The third section specifically
considers the relation of theory to practice in "international right." While
the concept of international right appears also as an element of Kant's
system of justice, in "Theory and Practice" Kant considers this form of
right from the perspective of individual duty, the duty of anyone as "a
member of a series of human generations." Kant maintains that there
is an "inborn duty of influencing posterity in such a way that it will
make constant progress" ... and that this duty may rightfully be handed
down from one generation to the next."[33] He further argues that hope
is necessary to the "earnest desire to do something useful for the common good."[34]

While practice follows principle in Kant's moral theory, the "inborn duty" of contributing to historical progress cannot be provided
with specific content without the assistance of reflective judgment.
The objectives of humanity as a whole cannot be intuitively grasped.
It is necessary therefore to attempt to "foresee" these objectives in terms
of actual projects that can be further perfected. This requires the judgment that such projects contribute toward progress, that progress in
history is possible. Without the belief in the natural capacity of the
human race to morally improve, Kant maintains, the attitude of even
right-thinking individuals would have to be to avoid involvement
with most men. Thus, our judgments that moral progress is possible in
the historical sphere support our cooperative endeavors in our personal moral lives.

Some commentators reject any attempt to introduce normative
concepts into the historical process and point to Kant's tendency to be
conservative or even skeptical concerning the relationship between
political and moral progress. Kant's skepticism is said to be due to his
suspicion that a just political condition could be achieved by "intelligent devils" operating entirely out of self-interest. If so, it is argued,
historical institutions constructed by such "intelligent devils" could
provide no evidence of moral progress, despite the apparent fit of
such institutions with the moral goal. This is because while we may be
uncertain about the moral quality of the intentions of individual human actors, any form of moral intention is ruled out by the internal
constitution and disposition of such devils. Strictly speaking, a devilish volition would recognize no constraints on individual interests

and would have no predisposition to the good or innate sociability. Lacking the appropriate predisposition, the achievements of such devils could not appear to them to have moral significance. Lacking the cognitive framework from which to project a moral world, devils could not imagine their achievements as the basis from which moral progress could arise. One has to wonder why, even if such beings were possible, Kant would ever use this situation to judge the value of human achievements, since in the *Religion* he explicitly rejects the concept of devilish volition as inappropriate to describe the human condition.

Kant's theory of moral evil proves illuminating precisely in the context of this debate about the nature and limits of historical progress. According to Kant, human beings may indeed adopt the principle of self–interest as their dominant incentive and become morally evil. But Kant defines "devilishness" as the complete elimination of the moral incentive, and he denies this is possible for a human being.[35] Furthermore, the predisposition to the good is an essential constituent of a human being and it is this predisposition which continuously orients our judgment, despite our personal failures, toward the morally possible. Kant's use of the "intelligent devil" model seems to be primarily intended as a kind of boost to the confidence of the observer of history that certain difficult tasks can be accomplished. It ceases to be appropriate when used to assess the significance of human accomplishments. Since the "intelligent devil" is basically a different species of being, it would not be wise to make inferences from this model concerning human history.[36]

That a general moral estimation of historical progress is "possible" does not of course make any particular estimation "plausible." That Kant believed that some evidence could be offered for particular estimations is demonstrated by his assessment of the "enthusiasm" and "moral sympathy" that is aroused in the "disinterested spectator" at the sight of significant political progress. The theoretical significance that Kant assigns to moral enthusiasm more than offsets the skepticism expressed in his remarks concerning the achievements of hypothetical "intelligent devils."

From the fact that those who have no immediate stake in the benefits of specific political reforms nonetheless rejoice in their occurrence Kant concludes that "a limited but unvarying" good will can be ascribed to human beings. It is "limited" because self–interest may continue to dominate the choices of particular agents, but "unvarying" because these judgments suggest the existence of genuine moral "aspirations" or a "moral predisposition" that can be counted among the factors that will influence historical development under the appropriate conditions. Van der Linden argues that the main value of the "moral enthusiasm" of these spectators is that it suggests a "moral commitment" that can become a motive for action under appropriate circumstances.[37] Atwell concludes that it is not the revolutionary actions that constitute the "event" disclosing the "moral predisposition" but rather it is the *publicly declared* revolutionary principles that mark the event. This shifts the focus of historical interpretation away from the particular and private and to the public realm.[38]

Thus, although revolutionary activity can fail to fulfill its promise, *republican principles as a public event*, once espoused and responded to, reveal a "capacity of the human race to be the cause of its own advance toward the better."[39] Even if the first such revolution were entirely due to the "cunning of nature," it is clear that Kant would not regard subsequent attempts to be merely such. Once such principles have been publicly acknowledged to "accord with right," we ought to regard further attempts to institute them as at least partly the product of the moral predisposition. Despite the fact that particular agents are not themselves morally good, and we are never in a position to judge this with certainty, the moral predisposition ensures that we are capable of choosing *appropriate actions for the right reasons.*[40] This is what is essential to our historical judgments, because this is what shapes the public consciousness that sustains historical progress.

The concept of an "enlightened public"[41] whose members freely exchange opinions even across national boundaries is critical not only for Kant's political philosophy but also for the very possibility of a philosophy of history. For it is only by means of a continuously existing learned public that history can be certified and transmitted and that the histories of peoples who are outside of the western tradition can, through expert translation, be brought into dialogue with it.[42] Thus Kant conceives of history as a story with a moral structure continuously generated and transmitted by a learned public.[43]

In one of the most focused examinations of Kant's philosophy of history, Yovel says that Kant's justification of his own Critical Philosophy entails the claim that rational consciousness develops historically and that once reason is aware of its own structure and principles, rationally motivated action is possible.[44] Thereafter it would seem that purely naturalistic explanations would require supplementation and that the historian would be justified in referring to conscious principles of action as factors in historical "explanation." The "cunning of nature" hypothesis would continue to provide valuable support to human efforts but would not displace reason's role in the evaluation and guidance of human action.

Although the intelligible nature of the moral predisposition as a rational incentive precludes its treatment as a principle of natural causality and renders its operation "undetermined with respect to time," Kant maintains that significant political events, identified through our reflective judgments, are "too much interwoven with the interest of mankind" to ever be forgotten.[45]

I believe this projection of an enduring interest in such events is meant to be more than a peculiar kind of empirical/historical speculation. This is an extrapolation of Kant's view of the ineradicable character of the moral incentive at the level of "pragmatic anthropology," and links Kant's philosophy of history more closely with the ethical conceptions worked out in the *Religion*.

Paralleling Kant's rejection of "devilish" volition in the *Religion*, this linking of anthropology and history underlies Kant rejection of the thesis of "moral terrorism"—the thesis that human history will become an unending decline into wickedness. Taking the peaceable federation of republics and the ethical commonwealth as the ultimate goals of history entails that historical development includes moral development. These goals depend upon an explicit commitment to social justice that cannot be expected to result from self-interest alone, however "intelligent." These goals define also the "critical" conception of the "highest good," which is the necessary object of a good disposition and upon which the validity of the moral law itself depends.

When fully analyzed, Kant's philosophy of history and ethics are deeply and systematically interconnected. The plurality of human cultures is a historical fact. I have argued that culture is an intrinsic expression of human freedom and that it is the task of practical reason to order and integrate the complex array of human purposes that result from cultural differentiation and development. This integration is possible and desirable only if history is conceived teleologically and there exists some means of orientation to guide human judgment and action. We have noted that an international or cosmopolitan community is required to make manifest and adjudicate the full range of human potentiality. This is the goal in terms of which particular political events are assessed The moral predisposition that recognizes and signifies these events in terms of their bearing on political evolution and international justice is the mechanism of orientation. Disinterested judgments make manifest this disposition and provide the means for a public discourse that is capable of taking on a cosmopolitan character. In the next section I shall discuss the importance of the public use of reason and the development of international or cosmopolitan publics as necessary stages of moral progress.

6

Cosmopolitan Publics, International Law, and Human Rights

In the previous chapter I have argued that judgments of purposiveness and political progress are linked to the public use of reason and ultimately to the development of a cosmopolitan public. In this chapter I would like to explore how a cosmopolitan public arises from the political and cultural pluralism that is the expression of practical freedom. In particular, I want to argue that the acceptance of this pluralism in the form of an international federation is not a "second-best" solution to the problem of peace. By this I mean that acceptance of this pluralism is not a pragmatic concession to the imperfect nature of man but has its own basis in the moral requirements of Kantian theory. I base this conclusion on the teleological principles implicit in Kant's ethics and philosophy of history. I will define a Kantian cosmopolitan condition as that set of international institutions designed to support the full range and development of human cultures that arise as a consequence of cultural pluralism. I will then demonstrate how cosmopolitanism is linked to the development of a form of international law embodying a positive theory of human rights.

In chapter 4 I considered how freedom, introduced by the development of reason, continuously creates cultural difference. Once we recognize that cultural differentiation is intrinsic to Kant's anthropology, it is clear that cultural pluralism is not an external constraint on moral development but a factor internal to this process. The teleology of freedom, the capacity to set ends, does not require an identity of material content among these ends. Quite the contrary, in explicating the duty of self-perfection Kant argues that a variety of specific skills

should be cultivated so that practical freedom will develop in a manner responsive to change and opportunity. Likewise, the perfection of
the species, according to Kant, requires a similar diversification of cultural talent so that the practical freedom of humanity will develop to
its highest capacity. These practical capacities, valuable in their own
right, are also the means to fulfill our moral duties, and since these
duties involve the whole of mankind, these capacities will have to take
on a cross-cultural and ultimately cosmopolitan character.

The interdependence between historical and moral development
is particularly compelling in the area of international law, human rights,
and the development of a cosmopolitan community. But what exactly
is a cosmopolitan community and what role does it play in the evolution of international law and human rights?

In "Idea for a Universal History from a Cosmopolitan Point of View,"
Kant foretells the development of a universal cosmopolitan condition
that "will come into being as the womb wherein all the original capacities of the human race can develop."[1] In support of this end, Kant
argues that nature has used cultural differences to curtail the development of a unified state which would stifle freedom and create a soulless despotism.[2] An early unification would also decrease the scope
and strength of cultural differentiation. These differences, associated
with a lively human freedom, are the seeds of the cosmopolitan condition to come.

On this view of history, culture both unites and divides. States are
originally created as mechanisms for the defense of a people's "way of
life." This originally unifies and protects a culture from external aggression. But armed political communities create the danger of continuous conflict that diminishes both internal cultural development
and cultural exchange. Because cosmopolitanism entails the perfection of *all original capacities of the species,* it cannot arise from a lawless
conflict of differences that would destroy or suppress some part of the
full legacy of the race. Nor can it arise as a consequence of cultural
isolation, for cultural development requires harmonious exchange. In
order for a "cosmopolitan condition" to develop from this political
and cultural pluralism, a lawful association of self-determining and
interacting polities must emerge. Kant therefore links the cosmopolitan condition to a free federation of republics united under a form of
international law that recognizes both the right of national self-determination and the right of all individuals as *citizens of the world* to interact and communicate.[3]

Kant thus associates cosmopolitanism with interaction between
individuals with different political (and often ethnic) identities. The
associative "rights" of these world citizens will constrain political insti-

tutions that otherwise would be primarily concerned with power and aggression to contribute toward intercultural development. Kant envisions a history of cultural contact and cultural change that does not lead to an eradication of difference but to a harmonious development of all cultural capacities.

"Idea" ends with the pronouncement that history will judge the value of any political association in terms of what it contributes to this final goal of global cultural development and perfection: "They will naturally value the history of earlier times . . . in answer to the question of what the various nations and governments have contributed to the goal of world citizenship and what they have done to damage it."[4]

Kant felt so strongly about this goal of world citizenship that in "Perpetual Peace" he made the "law of world citizenship", which would make this progressive cultural contact and change possible, the third of only three definitive articles, claiming that it was "indispensable for the maintenance of public human rights and hence also of perpetual peace."[5] I speak here of cultural change as well as cultural contact, because a global culture based upon human rights will require cultural evolution as different cultural traditions work out the implications of what it means to respect the human rights of others with whom they will be brought into lawful association.

Although limited to the conditions of "universal hospitality," the law of world citizenship is a powerful force for social–cultural change. Universal hospitality entails a right to associate, to travel, and to attempt communication with all the inhabitants of the earth. Concerning this universal right to associate, Kant explains:

> They have it by virtue of their common possession of the surface of the earth, where, as a globe, they cannot infinitely disperse and hence must finally tolerate the presence of each other. Originally, no one had more right than another to a particular part of the earth.[6]

These attempts to establish communication with others create patterns of trade and interaction that will gradually become accepted as elements of public law. These international codes of behavior provide a blueprint for an emerging "cosmopolitan condition" in which all persons will view themselves as citizens of the world as well as members of their cultures and nations.

Cultural pluralism, then, has a positive role to play in Kant's theory of world citizenship, from which emerges a form of universal human rights. Cultural difference challenges both our conception of "rights" and our conception of humanity, leading us to formulate principles of human right appropriate to a cosmopolitan condition. Cosmopolitan "right," the right to be treated with hospitality, is a basic form of human right. Although in one sense it is but a minimum condition of universal human rights, because it simply guarantees one a right to be a sojourner on this planet, cosmopolitan right in its applications to various forms of communication is also fundamental to the emergence of what James Bohman and others have called the "cosmopolitan public."[7] In "The Public Spheres of the World Citizen" Bohman presents pluralism as the necessary historical condition for the emergence of cosmopolitan right. This is because consciousness of this form of right arises only as a reflective judgment concerning the conditions necessary to resolve conflicts arising from political and cultural pluralism. Once articulated, cosmopolitan right provides the basis for forums of communication among individuals as members of the world community. By adopting the perspective of world citizens, individuals speak not just "as" and not just "for" the political interests of their fellow nationals but on behalf of the interests of humanity as such. The rights they promote are universal human rights.

T. M. McCarthy, in "Kant's Enlightenment Project Reconsidered," argues that the extension of Kant's enlightenment project to a global community requires a "multicultural universal discourse."[8] Both Bohman and McCarthy maintain that it is only in multicultural forms of discourse that the *unrestricted audience* required for the process of global enlightenment is available. Restricted audiences are defined by precommitments to specific goals and values. The distinction between restricted and unrestricted audiences is analogous to Kant's conception of the differences in the exercise of reason in private versus public contexts. Defining the private use of reason in "What is Enlightenment?" Kant says: "Private use I call that which one may make of it in a particular civil post or office which is entrusted to him."[9] In its private use, reason is constrained to a prior determination of the good, and the individual regards himself or herself as a part of a mechanism designed to further that end. Reason in this context is instrumental, not critical or reflective. But Kant argues that this need not obstruct enlightenment, because "so far as a part of the mechanism regards himself at the same time as a member of the whole community or of a society of world citizens and thus in the role of a scholar who addresses the public. . . . he certainly can argue."[10]

The use of reason to address the public defined as a whole community (even) of *world citizens* must be free to criticize any established belief or practice. This entails that cosmopolitan public opinion, especially as expressed by members of the more developed and politically liberal nations, may become critical of some of the social, political, and economic restrictions that some cultures attach to some social roles. Ascertaining whether such "restrictions" reflect fundamental values that are freely chosen or are the result of restraints imposed by material or political conditions not within the control of the group in question would require the kind of "deep understanding" that can only emerge in an open and reflective dialogue between members of cultural systems with differing values. If, however, the social system that is under criticism is deeply authoritarian, a critique of such restrictions may cause a withdrawal from interaction with parts of the cosmopolitan community. Are such withdrawals justified?

In "What is Enlightenment?" Kant addresses the issue of mankind's gradual emergence from "tutelage," which is not defined as natural but as "self-incurred." "Self-incurred is this tutelage when its cause lies not in lack of reason but in lack of resolution and courage to use it without direction from another."[11] By including the human tendency to rely on the opinions of others in the definition of "self-incurred" tutelage, Kant foregrounds the social context of the problem of human enlightenment. The duty of enlightenment is a form of the duty of self-perfection. Thus, it is a duty of virtue for which there is a latitude in performance. As with other duties of self-perfection, it is a duty that the individual may postpone, "but only for a time." Moreover, Kant maintains that it cannot be renounced. The explanation of why a duty that appears to be self-regarding cannot properly be renounced is quite interesting. While in one sense enlightenment is a development of one's own rational capacities, Kant's defense of this duty goes beyond the consequences for the individual, connecting personal to social development. The individual may not properly renounce enlightenment because to "renounce it for himself and even more to renounce it for posterity is to injure and trample on the rights of mankind."[12]

To understand what is at stake here, we must universalize the negative. When the individual renounces the development of his rational capacities "for himself alone," he is undermining his capacity to set ends and contradicting his nature as an end setter But the individual is also part of a social community that exists only in and through individuals. Should the individual completely renounce her rational development, she also quite literally diminishes the life of the social community. In fact, it is Kant's view that no individual is capable of meaningful rational development except in the context of a community. In universalizing her own case of renunciation, the individual not only violates her own nature as an end but also undermines the initial conditions for the development of anyone's rational capacity by reducing the available social capital.

The development of one's rational capacities is necessary for engagement in the critical dialogue of public social life. If it were morally
permissible for all persons to close themselves off from the public
sphere, from the ability to communicate from open perspectives, the
cosmopolitan public would not be a practical historical objective. Such
actions would "make a period of time fruitless in the progress of mankind toward improvement."[13] There is a duty of enlightenment in the
form of a duty to develop one's own reason. The duty to develop one's
own reason is a duty of self-perfection. Because the duty of enlightenment is not limited to the welfare of already existing persons, it is a
duty that can be extended to the social, political, and cultural institutions that individuals create. In "What is Enlightenment?" Kant considers a case of collective action that would place certain aspects of
group identity beyond discussion. In analyzing the decision of a society of clergyman to obligate themselves and their members by oath
"to a certain unchangeable symbol," Kant declares with unmistakable
clarity and directness that this cannot be made legitimate, even if sanc-
tioned by the civil law. He says:

> Such a contract, made to shut off all further enlighten-
> ment from the human race, is absolutely null and void even if
> confirmed by the supreme power, by parliament, and by the
> most ceremonious of peace treaties. . . . An age cannot bind
> itself. . . . That would be a crime against human nature . . . and
> the descendants would be fully justified in rejecting those de-
> crees.[14]

Reflecting on Kant's statements concerning the duty of enlightenment, I would conclude that while individuals and therefore presumably groups could "postpone" enlightenment, perhaps in the interest
of meeting more pressing needs, to attempt to renounce one's duty by
creating institutional mechanisms to shut off future communication is
not morally acceptable. While the attempt to maintain openness
through coercive means is self-defeating, since the imposition of beliefs violates autonomy by definition, we ought to protest the restric-
tion of communication in any form, whether legally or culturally imposed, as a violation of human, not merely individual, rights. In its
public use, reason seeks an unrestricted audience. Given that even
nations have a particular and therefore restricted character, reason will
naturally seek the society of world citizens. The full extension of public reason, then, creates a cosmopolitan condition.

Although the ability to step back and engage in critical-reflective
discourse concerning the justifiability of established beliefs and prac-

tices is always a matter of degree, dependent upon social, cultural, and psychological conditions, the existence of multicultural publics promotes this reflexivity by bringing to public awareness a diversity of reasonable but different conceptions of the good. These articulated differences have far-reaching effects upon the processes of cultural reproduction, social integration and identity formation facilitating cultural exchange and development. Arguing that most large nations today are already politically pluralistic and multicultural internally, Bohman envisions a plurality of overlapping and interlocking publics that transcend ethnic and political boundaries forming the basis for innovation, change, and the development of cooperative solutions to international problems. Because this public is by definition unrestricted and inclusive, it has the capacity to be self-reflexive and self-critical, questioning even its own past assumptions and bringing to public awareness the operation of parochialism and authority over its own political discourse. Publicly disclosed biases result in the emergence of new publics who compete for the allegiance of the public at large. When this happens, newly formed coalitions press established institutions for recognition or create new institutions that compete for inclusion. Continuously crossing constructed boundaries, Bohman envisions the dynamics of cosmopolitan publics as a process without a specific location in space or time.

An international or cosmopolitan public thus represents the most diverse and pluralistic of all publics. As such, it provides the broadest possible forum for exchange of arguments and perspectives. This is the audience that must also test, criticize, and limit the political strategies of the sovereign nations within a federation. While maintaining that the right to argue does not dispense with the requirements of civil order, specifically the requirement to obey the established rule of law, Kant viewed enlightenment as the product of a process of progressive change. Critique could guide this change in a progressive manner because, according to Kant, enlightenment entails a commitment to the good resulting from increased understanding, which "must step by step ascend the throne and influence the principles of government."[15] In other words Kant expected that enlightenment would result in an improved moral condition of the people. Their commitment to the good (articulated in public debate) would, regardless of the historical form of government, eventually impact and transform the nature of government itself. While we cannot expect a steady growth of enlightenment without its constitutional supports, moral improvement is not a simple top-down affair. Legislative authority is always for Kant a "representative" function, but the public realm of debate provides the touchstone of its legitimacy. And in the public realm, reason ought to be completely unrestricted. When the enlightenment project is re-conceived in terms of cosmopolitan publics, the influence brought to bear on national politics, stemming from improved moral insight on the part of the peoples of the world, is translated into an improved international politics. Thus, it is not the structure of international government alone that will bring about perpetual peace but that which is to develop within it, the cosmopolitan public. It is this public that will provide the evolving content of international law that organized political leadership will then inscribe into its structures.

Because a free federation is conditioned upon a right of national self–determination, the role of the cosmopolitan public is extremely important in a Kantian international system. Without the guidance of a cosmopolitan public, a free federation might become a closed system of hostile or at least indifferent nations. In virtue of their civil constitutions, which express for each people their own conception of "right," members of the federation are "sovereign" and have outgrown the requirement of submission to coercive law. Their adherence to the federation therefore must be "free" and their constitutions free from interference. Without the authority to legislate the content of civil right, an international federation can only prohibit aggression, require that its members maintain a republican form of the rule of law (which does entail basic human rights), abide by the conditions of universal hospitality, and *respect the terms of their own agreements*. The function of a cosmopolitan public is then to promote the extension of the terms of international agreements to include a broader range of human rights that will facilitate development and sustain peaceable association. This is the long–term function of a cosmopolitan public, but it must develop its agenda from an inherently pluralistic political basis and must deal with the conflicts that diversity will sometimes entail.

Beyond the requirements stated above, a free federation admits a plurality of political ends that may result in somewhat different systems of positive law. Beyond the basic human right of equal protection of the law (a requirement of the republican form of government), what the law guarantees to whom may differ from state to state. In *Human Rights and Human Diversity*, A. J. Milne attempts to deal with the challenges that cultural diversity provides to a theory of universal human rights and the implications for international relations. Milne argues that human rights derive from the requirements of social life irrespective of the form it may take. As such, human rights describe a minimum but universal standard that sets moral limits to the scope of cultural diversity without denying the role that culture plays in shaping an individual's social identity.[16] Because the universal moral standard is compatible with a wide range of cultural diversity, human rights, according to Milne, must be contextualized. Contextualization of rights, he argues, is an appropriate extension of the recognition that rights are dependent upon a societal context and that social structures vary from culture to culture. Social stratification may result in differences in the scope and content of civil rights even within a particular state. But, Milne maintains, as long as these status positions arise from some division of labor that is in the best interest of the community as a whole and are widely accepted by that community, what is "fair" and "equal" under the law will be relative to these positions. However, he concludes, in the spirit of Kantian philosophy, that every society must guarantee to each member the possibility of a way of life compatible with human dignity.

Because difference is inevitable and fundamental to an individual's social identity, Milne argues that taking diversity seriously requires noninterference in the internal affairs of others. Noninterferences is on his account both a pragmatic and a moral requirement of relationships between nations. Although Milne's position allows for the recognition of minimal and universal human rights on the part of a cosmopolitan public, this recognition would appear to be irrelevant in an international politics bound by the principle of noninterference, for it would not allow for direct enforcement of human rights by the international community. Although Milne's account is not explicitly Kantian and so is not meant to be applied to a specifically Kantian form of federation, his conclusions appear to be in line with traditional interpretations of Kant's theory, which maintain that the principle of noninterference permits extensive violations of human rights in the interests of peace. However, how one responds to the potential dilemma created by a conflict between a violation of human rights and a possible intervention to end it depends upon how one defines the "internal affairs of others." Are violations of human rights simply a matter of the "internal affairs" of the members of a Kantian federation?

Although Milne is reluctant to invest the international community with even a limited right of interference, for reasons that are ultimately more pragmatic than moral, violations of human dignity are clearly outside the arena of justified cultural difference as even he understands it. From a Kantian perspective, such violations are not merely "internal" matters, because they undermine the idea of human dignity that is the basis of the moral duty of respect for cultural difference and autonomy. As a moral principle, noninterference is derived from this basis. Milne's common good defense of differential social status does not permit individuals to be viewed as mere "means" to the ends of others but must be rooted in a view of differences that sustain the dignity of each social position.[17] This entails that the community will not be polarized or in a state of serious political conflict.

There can be, then, no ethical defense of cultural or political rules that deny individuals social standing and some form of participation in the common good. If, as a result of the cultural beliefs of a dominant group, some members of a community are denied protection of law and social standing compatible with human dignity, so much the worse for those cultural beliefs. Political interference on the part of the world community may be justified.[18] Interventions of this kind are not "cultural impositions" but judgments of the world community that the basic conditions of law necessary for standing in the federation are lacking. While Kant's conception of republicanism covers a variety of forms of government and therefore allows limited active participation in the making of laws, equality and rights pertain to anyone "subject" to the law. In "On the Relationship of Theory to Practice in Political Right" Kant explains man's equality as a subject in the following terms:

> But all who are subject to laws are the subjects of a state, and are thus subject to the right of coercion along with all other members of the commonwealth. . . . But if there were two persons exempt from coercion, neither would be subject to coercive laws, and neither could do to the other anything contrary to right, which is impossible.[19]

Rules that deny subjects any civil standing or rights before the law are ethically null and void, and so do not qualify as laws that must not be interfered with.

It has been argued that, given Kant's absolute prohibition on revolution, all civil resistance or political intervention is unjustified. However, the relation between sovereign and citizen is such that actions that would destroy the civil standing of subjects by denying subjects the basic protections of law would also place these subjects in the state of nature or war. Arbitrary uses of power cannot be acts of sovereignty. In such cases (non)subjects have at least the rights of nature. They need not "submit" to their own destruction. Do the citizens of other nations then have the right to assist subjects at war with their sovereign? Would the recognition of the right to assist or intervene violate the terms of a Kantian federation and undermine the ultimate goal of peace? On what grounds might the citizens of other nations intervene on behalf of those left unprotected by civil law?

It can be argued that harms done to those who are denied legal standing in their own communities are harms done to the international community. Violations of human right are not just harms done to individuals but are also harms done to the community. Even within civil society, the harm done to the individual when a right is violated is not rectified simply by compensation to the individual, nor can the individual waive the right of the community to address the general harm.[20] So too, the harm done to the subjects of particular nations when they are denied appropriate legal standing is not simply an internal matter of civil law. Placed in a state of nature, the wider or international community becomes their community of aid. Even in the state of nature we have moral obligations of assistance to those in distress.

Therefore it would seem that insofar as sovereign powers act against the basic human rights of their subjects, their title to be exempt from interference is forfeited. That interference in the "internal affairs" of a sovereign nation may be justified by the principle of human rights does not tell us exactly when or in what manner it may in fact become a moral duty. Interference may be at great cost to the legitimate interests of would-be benefactors and, as with all duties of aid, such considerations may be weighed.[21] But violations of human right are never justified by cultural beliefs or political power. Interventions to prevent them cannot be prohibited on such grounds. According to Kant a hindrance to a hindrance to freedom is just. And ultimately civil law must accord with international law, or the "structure of all the others will unavoidably be undermined and must finally collapse."[22]

How then do societies with substantially different ways of life interact as members of an international community?[23] An organized international community is needed to reduce conflicts between distinct communities and thereby preserve the integrity of different ways of life. But is maintaining peace then the only purpose or obligation of an international community? What is the relationship between peace, diversity, and human rights? Since the relationship of individuals of one society to those of another is clearly not a local matter, for an international association to be both *peaceable and progressive* in its interactions there must be recognized standards for the human rights of individuals as members of the world community. Some form of international law is required not only to specify the rights of nations in relation to other nations but the rights of individuals as *world citizens*. The rights of individuals may first be articulated as a response to our rights to associate, but once articulated they cannot but be reflectively applied as universal human rights. As universal human rights they cannot be violated by any government, including one's own. Thus, if I have a right as a world citizen not to be arbitrarily killed, then I have that right as a traveler and as a subject of a particular state. Efforts on the part of representatives at the recent international conference in Rome to establish a World Court with the power to try government officials for mass killings and rapes reflect this attempt to articulate a standard for the rights of individuals as world citizens.[24] These types of crimes have occurred largely in the context of ethnic conflict. The concept of a crime that has international standing because it is a "crime against humanity"—in which one's humanity is denied precisely because of one's ethnic identity—illustrates the important connection between human rights and cultural identity within the world community.

Political pluralism can become "cosmopolitan" only if an international federation adopts, in addition to its postulate of state autonomy, the human rights of individuals in relation to states and to other individuals in other communities. While state autonomy may at first appear to be in conflict with this admission of human rights, we have seen that cosmopolitan right is an essential component of this form of association, which aims at enduring development and peace. Cosmopolitanism depends upon a universal right of association, giving all of its members, individually and collectively, a stake in the future of the federation. Without this the federation would be but a loose association of relatively closed societies, unprepared to protect against internal dissolution or a sudden act of aggression. This stake in the whole is what Kant's third definitive article for the establishment of a free federation, so modest in its statement, seeks to establish. Noting that the development of a community of peoples will result in a "violating of rights in one place . . . felt throughout the world,"[25] the ability to register this distress, enter into dialogue about its causes and remedies and recommend change is essential to the sense of a common stake in the future of the federation.

In his lectures entitled "Human Rights in the Modern World," delivered in 1948,[26] Arthur Holcombe credits Kant for having discovered in his principle of "universal hospitality" the key to the formula of international rights. Holcombe recognized in this simple formula the power of communication between the different peoples and their representatives in the United Nations to bring forth in time a global human–rights culture. He argued that the principal task of the newly formed United Nations should be to define the relationship of the individual to international society in the form of an international bill of rights that "would deal with that part of the general field of human rights that is concerned with the relations between persons in different countries and between such persons and the general international organization itself."[27]

Arguing that it would be a mistake to try to regulate the relations between the peoples of individual states and their own government to a greater extent than is necessary for the purpose of securing greater freedom in the relations between different peoples, Holcombe cites with approval the declaration of the General Assembly that freedom of information is the "touchstone" of all the freedoms to which the United Nations is dedicated. He praises early efforts to secure the rights of journalists to gather and disseminate news everywhere. Since we cannot all acquaint ourselves at first hand with the diversity of cultural conditions, promoting protection for the work of journalists throughout the world gives practical expression to the ideal of "hospitality" and the right of association. Through the dissemination of information, journalists support a cosmopolitan condition and provide a means for the disclosure and registering of distress at the violation of human rights.

While this approach to human rights has been criticized as stressing the western preference for "negative freedoms," the recognition and elaboration of positive rights depend heavily for their effectiveness and implementation on the cosmopolitan public's ability to communicate the impact of differing cultural and economic conditions on human welfare. Without this information, international strategies for the promotion of human welfare cannot be developed. Free dissemination of information promotes the cross–cultural dialogue essential to the extension of the human–rights agenda.

Thus, while we can expect some form of human rights to emerge from the structure of international association itself, we must also expect, as argued earlier, that cultural context will provide differences in the way that rights are specified within different states. In order to accord with the emphasis upon the value of group identity basic to many cultures, democratic values and process must also be justified in terms that are not founded exclusively upon western notions of individual autonomy. Thus, in upholding the importance of democratic institutions, one should not assume that human rights are focused narrowly on the individual in abstraction from any form of group identity. Recognizing this potential conflict between democratic "majoritarianism" and minority rights both within and between cultures, Follesdal argues for a normative political theory that can incorporate the value of cultural belonging while embracing the desirability of cultural change. In particular, he notes that culture is not static and that development may cause cultural change. Explaining the function of group identity in fostering democratic processes, Follesdal states:

> The role of cultural membership grounds claims based on the interest of members to influence the institutional causes of change. A large problem of members of traditional ethnic national groups,

as well as other minorities, is their need to develop their culture
to cope with and exploit new modes of life.[28]

Democratic process, on this view, is valuable not because it is a
western invention or part of a liberal normative political theory, but
because it allows participants in a particular culture to direct change
along desirable paths and in ways that can protect their basic values.
In defending a right to cultural integrity, Follesdal maintains that it is
not necessary to assume that every aspect of a given culture is desirable. Deep structural change, such as extending the franchise to women,
may be necessary to ensure participation in the political processes
that shape social and cultural institutions. Active political participation is desirable to ensure that social institutions are not adversely
impacted by forces external to the culture but are guided in their development from within. Without this ability to direct development
from within, vulnerable cultures may be marginalized and suffer economic decline. Thus their "autonomy" will be attained only at the cost
of their human development. Growth in appreciation for the value of
democratic institutions in protecting cultural integrity should be expected to lead to some structural change, but cannot justify the complete assimilation of minority cultures by majorities or the wholesale
replication of western social formations in nonwestern cultures. A global
ethics will understand democracy as the self-determination of groups
of individuals, with specific cultural identities engaged in an ongoing
process of development.
   It is important to recognize also that differences in how rights are
specified are not independent of the economic, political, and social
structures of a given society and that these structures are themselves
affected by interactions with the international community. Therefore
the role of the international or "cosmopolitan public" cannot be limited to criticism of unacceptable policies within particular nations. In
addition, such publics will have to adopt a constructive role in shaping how nations formulate international strategies for economic, political, and social change. In particular, the policies of more powerful
nations, which have the greatest impact on the course of development, must be open to review by the public at large. Through public
scrutiny, cosmopolitan publics can bring these policies into greater
harmony with the interests of the entire international community, thus
influencing the way in which international law itself is formulated.
This continuous criticism and review is necessary in order to give to
the maxims of international law the affirmative form of public law
that Kant claims is the test for the ultimate compatibility of politics
and morality, "All maxims which stand in need of publicity in order

not to fail their end agree with politics and right combined."[29] What can be attained *only through publicity* in the affirmative sense of seeking the broad agreement of the public at large not only supports the end of making the public "satisfied" with its condition; most importantly, it removes distrust in the maxims of politics by securing their conformity to the "rights of the public."

At the level of cosmopolitan publics, this broad agreement is the most difficult to accomplish and maintain. Recognizing these difficulties, Bohman argues that we must give up the idea that such agreement is contingent upon an identity of ends. Rather, we must view such agreement as aimed at the conditions under which a plurality of persons can inhabit a common public space. Using the multicultural experience of the United States as an example, McCarthy argues that this agreement may have to be limited to the procedures and processes that result in the resolution of reasonable "disagreement." Only in and through the democratic character of social institutions can such "reasonable disagreement" reach the level of accommodation and compromise needed to sustain a complex public order. With federative institutions providing the democratic structure for an international civil society, Bohman envisions innovations as beginning within non-governmental organizations and experimental voluntary associations. These groups in turn create informal and cooperative links among multiple publics, thereby establishing the communicative networks necessary for the participation of all citizens in global planning.

When organized around international deliberative institutions, a public sphere of democratically organized associations could, Bohman argues, shift the location of sovereignty back to citizens.[30] The power of global corporations to effect cultural homogenization could be balanced by a cosmopolitan community self-consciously committed to its own diversity. Such a community could in turn influence the character and goals of global corporations. These citizens would be world citizens not because they lack a cultural or social identity but because they are willing to bring that identity to bear on an evolving world order. Cosmopolitanism is then not antithetical to, but a condition of, genuine cultural pluralism. Pluralism in the sense of the participation of all peoples in building a world order in which all of the cultural capacities of humanity are brought to perfection is best realized by international agreements which "must step by step ascend" from an enlightened cosmopolitan public and finally "influence the principles of government."

With cultural difference at the basis of historical development, a pluralistic political federation under international law appears to be the form this history must take *for reasons intrinsic to the Kantian conception of right.* This international federation, in turn, is necessary to the development of a cosmopolitan public space. It is only in terms of a cosmopolitan public space that the concept of "right" can be freed from its parochial connotations and become adequate to secure civil and social rights that accord with human dignity. It is no wonder, then, that Kant sets a "universal cosmopolitan condition" as the goal of his universal history and concludes that the value of political development is in "what the various nations and governments have contributed to the goal of world citizenship."[31]

Conclusion:
History and the Moral
Duties of Individuals

One of the most striking criticisms of Kant's philosophy of history is that if one accepts the possibility of historical moral development, history then appears as a process that treats earlier generations as mere means to the ends of later generations. It is claimed that such a process is ethically corrupt, because it would violate the moral equality of all men. Later generations would lead an easier moral life and would reap the moral benefits of the work and sufferings of earlier generations. An unfair distribution of moral benefits and burdens would result, which runs counter to the proportionality of virtue and happiness envisioned in the idea of the highest good.

Implicit in this complaint is the assumption that the removal of obstacles to the realization of certain moral tasks automatically results in a greater degree of virtue for individuals. However, since the Kantian conception of virtue requires more than externally good behavior and this something more must involve an act of freedom, whatever moral improvement occurs cannot be the automatic result of the work of others. This much the critic of historical development is likely to concede. But an appearance of unfairness persists that must be addressed. If greater "happiness" results, it must somehow be earned.[1]

Moral tasks, I would maintain, are shaped by the historical process and are different for different generations. The external institutions that provide the basis of civil right and peaceable economic and political interactions among nations are in constant need of modification and adjustment if they are to accord with justice. Kant recognized that while certain institutional arrangements could be judged as morally

101

preferable to others, the process of producing a universal cosmopolitan condition is historically open-ended. In "An Old Question Raised
Again," taking note of the issues of orientation and scope Kant carefully crafts his proposition on progress in the following terms.

> The human race has always been in progress toward the bet-
> ter and will continue to be so henceforth. To him who does
> not consider what happens in just some one nation but also
> has regard to the whole scope of all the peoples on earth who
> will gradually come to participate in progress, this reveals the
> prospect of an immeasurable time.[2]

This passage suggests that while some institutional arrangements
can be considered indicators of progress, the creation and extension of
such institutions is an active-participative process inclusive of all
peoples and all generations yet to come. The sociocultural as well as
economic-political dimensions of this participation will require a
flexible and creative approach to institutional development. When
viewed in its full complexity the work of historical institutional development is not a consequence of the automatic transference of the work
of one generation to the benefit of another. Each generation must create its own moral world order.

In fact, one might argue that the moral life of later generations is
in some respects more challenging than the moral life of earlier generations. As the scope and complexity of institutional life grows, the
need for an educated and enlightened public increases. Where social-
cultural opportunities for such enlightenment are present, the individual has a stronger obligation to participate and to maintain these
conditions for future generations. This sense of a stronger obligation
on the part advancing cultures is suggested in the following passage
from "Perpetual Peace":

> Hence providence is justified in the history of the world, for
> the moral principle in man is never extinguished, while with
> advancing civilization reason grows pragmatically in its ca-
> pacity to realize ideas of law. But at the same time the culpa-
> bility for the transgression also grows.[3]

It is a generally accepted implication of the Kantian concept of
duty that what we cannot do, we are not obligated to do. But the
converse is also true. What we can do to promote the realization of
moral value, we ought to do. As reason "grows pragmatically" in its
ability to produce institutions of moral value, duties to sustain these

institutions arise. Failure to act to sustain such institutions is then morally culpable.

How does the achievement of certain moral goals in the form of the instantiation of specific institutions of moral value such as democratic republican governments and international law affect contemporary moral duties? I would maintain that the civil liberty that the subjects of democratic republican governments enjoy carries with it obligations of greater scope and of a stricter character. In particular, those who enjoy a high degree of civil liberty have obligations to develop and maintain the public discourse required for the enlightenment of public life. Contemporary democratic publics have achieved a degree of self-consciousness concerning this task, especially as it affects the quality of public institutions and the quality of information received through the press and other media. Debates concerning how public institutions delivering education should be structured to achieve equality of access and opportunity, how curricula should be structured to enhance the performance of different groups, and even how the diversity of values within our civic culture should be represented illustrate the growing self-conscious character of this process.

In an increasingly global society, civil liberty provides the opportunity, and so carries with it the broad duty, to promote the existence of cosmopolitan publics generally. Citizens of democratic governments have obligations to advance understanding of human rights and to contribute to the economic development of other nations. Through their voluntary associations they have obligations to cooperate with like-minded citizens of other nations in the advancement of moral goals and in the articulation of international standards of justice.

These are, in a sense, collective duties. They define duties in a social sphere that go beyond individual to individual duty. It is the social-historical context that defines the scope of such duties, and it is the individual's relation to that social context that determines the nature of one's moral contribution. We have argued that moral progress has a social and cultural as well as a legal institutional dimension. Social-cultural communities have ethical dimensions and can set collective moral tasks for their members.

What is the nature of the social union that grounds our collective duties? Some types of institutional reform are grounded in our civil commitments. But we have argued that the level of institutional reform necessary for a cosmopolitan community cannot be limited to civil life. Justice must be a feature of the entire international community. In "Idea," eighth thesis, Kant argues that peace and well-ordered international relations are necessary to provide the resources and opportunity to direct civil energy to true education and civil enlightenment.

But for peace and international order to be more than episodic it is necessary, in addition to internal improvements, to think in terms of civil efforts directed toward the wider cosmopolitan community. Problems of international economic development and human rights will have to be addressed for international order to be sustained.[4]

Social life, of course, exists in a material and economic context as well as in a legal one, and issues of justice and human rights cannot ultimately be disconnected from issues of economic development. Economic development touches upon our relationship to the material world, which we collectively utilize to satisfy human needs and purposes. What are our duties to the nonhuman world from which our economic and material resources are derived? Thomas Auxter argues that the task of reason is to create a moral teleological order. But in so doing, he notes that reason does not create the value of things. To assume otherwise, to assume that reason's role is to subdue nature as an object that is without any intrinsic character, is to set humanity onto a course in conflict with nature. That such conflict is inherent in the purely instrumentalist attitude toward material ends found in early liberalism is also the point of Velkley's critique. In recognizing that a moral teleology must respect the purposive character of human social existence in its natural context, we are led to the construction of an ecological model for our interaction with the material world. In arguing for understanding Kantian ethics in the context of an immanent as opposed to a transcendent teleology, Auxter notes that a transcendent telos may hinder the development of values not related to the dominant end. Purposiveness as a nonmetaphysical value inherent in human experience is a more appropriate guide for an ecological praxis.

> An immanent teleology, on the other hand, allows for a plurality of diverse experiences to be realized because it allows for experience of the patterns in nature to be a factor in deciding how value is to be understood and developed in practical terms. . . . Whereas a transcendent teleology is a rationale for conscripting nature . . . an immanent teleology is a justification for mutual adaptation.[5]

Mutual adaptation requires sustaining the community of interacting natural entities. Sustainability is the guiding theme of ecology and of the emerging field of ecological economics, which includes the effects of our interaction with our environment in its analysis of value. Sustainability concerns not only the integrity of our environmental context but also the viability of any future economic "growth." If we are obligated to improve conditions for persons in underdeveloped nations and to provide the same for future generations, we will need to formulate definitions of improvement and means of growth that respect the integrity of the natural environment. To fail to do so will simply accelerate the degradation of both the quality and quantity of available resources. This in turn will exacerbate the conflicts over scarce resources, which will become scarcer as the environment continues to be degraded. We need therefore an ecological economics as the basis for just and sustainable economic development. Only an ecological economics can provide for the balanced development that will bring all nations into a condition of harmonious sustainable growth. This model should guide the development of new technologies adaptive to the purposive patterns of material existence.

For an ecological model to flourish, the social dynamic that views human ends as only instrumental to the achievement of material goods must be transformed. The instrumental framework cannot overcome the higher-order conflicts that necessarily arise from different human ends in relation to a finite material world. An instrumentalist attitude is also an ingredient in the subordination of the moral law to the incentives of self-interest. The attempt to apply the instrumentalist framework to our social interactions degrades the quality of our social practices and institutions. Insofar as this instrumental framework is a manifestation of the corruption of our capacity for moral reasoning, a transformation in our mode of thinking, interacting, and willing is required. This need for a fundamental transformation in social practice points to the limitations inherent in the traditional forms of economic and political analysis and the need for a transfusion of moral values into social theorizing.

While political reform is undoubtedly necessary, especially to secure and increase the scope for an enlightened public to develop, states alone cannot be expected to effect this transformation. With increasing international order, states can be expected to gradually grasp the consequences of economic interdependence for their own security. Yet their concerns for truly cosmopolitan objectives can be expected to be generally limited to the disruptive impacts that conflict may have for their own security and well-being. This means that without the concurrent development of an enlightened public, state policies are likely to focus on conflict suppression rather than on the universal development required for genuine and lasting peace. It becomes the task of enlightened publics to demand that policies designed to address international conflicts include strategies for the improvement of human rights. To secure the implementation of human rights, international order and peace must be founded on principles that strengthen rather than weaken the capacity for economic and civic development.

As noted earlier, Bohman argues that an international order based upon federation is not sufficient to create perpetual peace. But he also argues that a federative framework fosters the development of a cosmopolitan public that can limit and shape the strategic aims of states in such a way as to promote perpetual peace.[6]

This is because, Bohman notes, most nation states already contain within themselves pluralist publics. Pluralism is essential to the development of a cosmopolitan public, because the idea of cosmopolitan right emerges in the process of reflection upon the conflicts that pluralism entails. Through the public use of reason within pluralist publics, citizens can come to awareness of the conditions that restrict and limit consensus. The public can become concerned with its own "character" and moral improvement.

The interaction between the public and its existing institutions and bureaucracies is notoriously difficult and complex. The latter tend toward conservative solutions and to nondecisions. When impasses occur, new publics develop and a contest for general public opinion emerges that can modify existing institutions. Institutions that do not respond to these changes in public opinion lose their legitimacy and this may lead to open challenges and fundamental change. While many a politician bemoans the changing character of public opinion, the idea of right at stake in these public debates is a vehicle for a more inclusive understanding of justice and human welfare.

In that the scope of these issues is ultimately international, the form of community necessary to address these issues must have some basic commitment to humanity as such, a commitment going beyond one's own cultural and civic group. Such a community is not a merely "national" community. We have noted how a cosmopolitan community first arises within a civil community on the basis of questions transcending one's particular or private sphere. By questioning whether certain rights or liberties pertain merely to the individual or to the family, to one gender or to one sexual orientation, one constructs a perspective that moves beyond what is particular to one's self. In "Community, Immortality, and Enlightenment," Alfred Nordmann notes that Kant's essay on enlightenment was a contribution to a larger debate that was in part prompted by the question of whether marriage should be considered merely a civil contract or should continue to require for its legitimacy the ceremonial rites of a church. Nordmann argues that this debate "in effect negotiated the boundaries between private and public spheres." He maintains that it is implicit in Kant's view that "in the course of enlightenment, more and more of the doctrines considered binding in the private sphere are taken up and clarified within the public sphere, and thus more and more of the private life becomes assimilated into the exchanges of a critical audience."[7]

At issue is the question whether critical reason should set limits to the process of enlightenment or allow that all aspects of human experience fall into its range. Nordmann notes that Kant, in referring to his own transitional age of enlightenment, called it "the age of true criticism to which everything must be subjected."[8]

An enlightened public then must gradually absorb issues that begin in the private sphere but that ultimately pertain to our collective social existence. Through our reflective public judgments we must orient ourselves amid our differences to find a form of freedom that allows a multiplicity of morally appropriate ends to flourish. Republican governments provide the best conditions for the development of an enlightened public that can then use its enlarged understanding to address its differences with other cultural and political groups.

Since a merely formal process of legal right will not provide the substantive content that human right requires, we must look to what Philip Rossi has called "the social authority of reason" to indicate what concrete social practices are required to establish the external or public form of a moral community.[9] Rossi maintains that Kant's theory of political authority is not meant to provide a complete account of the principles governing external human conduct. He argues that

> even as Kant marks out the domain of public political authority he does not hereby make it coextensive . . . with the entire set of conditions which constitute that "external" order. . . . We may term the authority which employs such non-coercive means to govern human conduct in the external order "social authority."[10]

As Rossi notes, it is important to recognize that Kant's view of moral progress depends upon the fulfillment of two sets of interdependent conditions. One set of conditions refers to the motivation and intention to work for moral progress; and, as I argued in chapter 3, this intention involves both the act of "individual conversion" and the setting of a universal social goal. The second set of conditions refers to the shaping of human sociocultural practices to provide a context within which moral motivation and intention can be effective. Just political structures are a necessary but not a sufficient condition of a morally effective social order. In particular, human social dynamics need to be infused with the "social authority" of reason in order to overcome the effects of "radical evil" and provide the coordination of efforts that marks a moral community.

I have argued that insofar as radical evil infects human social dynamics, it is only by means of transforming the existing social dynamic that the power of evil can be lessened. The purification of this dynamic requires that interaction be based upon the social respect exemplified in the noncoercive exercise of public reason. In order to form institutions that mirror this respect, we must be able to come to understand the ends of others and to form social institutions based upon diversity. Only a cosmopolitan politics based upon the public use of reason can protect this diversity and give it institutional expression. It is neither necessary nor desirable to expect a homogenization of ends. Solutions to complex problems must be based on a pluralist consensus and upon cooperative associations.

These cooperative or ethical associations must cut across national boundaries. Voluntary associations formed to promote the basic interests and rights of world citizens are social instantiations of ethical communities. Ethical communities need not be limited to communities of religious faith, although they often do in fact arise from such communities. Kant maintains that ethical communities can only arise on the basis of civil communities. We can also see that in order for ethical communities to fully promote universal ends, they must address the concerns of citizens of other states and so in this sense the goals of the ethical community presuppose an international legal order that at least minimally and provisionally expresses the interests of other communities.

As the social power to shape and reform legal institutions, ethical communities exist in a dynamic and reflexive relationship with political communities. Ethical communities are not anarchic. They are committed to the idea and possibility of just political frameworks. There is a convergence in aims between the cosmopolitan public and the ethical community. According to Kant, ecclesiastical religions or churches are only vehicles of ethical community. The idea of an ethical community can be extended beyond organized religious groups to include all voluntary associations of persons publicly committed to the promotion of universal human interest. This public commitment is the "historical" or temporal expression of social union under a principle of virtue. What makes such a social unity possible, enduring, and capable of a progressive inclusion of multiple ethical communities is, according to Kant, a form of practical faith in a moral order that is not itself a merely human artifact.

Because the scope of radical evil is universal, the moral goal or highest good is an inherently social and historical project. Kant's moral project has religious dimensions because the scope of the social project and the nature of the social union go beyond what merely cultural, economic, or material conditions of human existence can produce. Because the social goal is fully universal, it must encompass the cultural-material conditions of human life, including the full scope of the appropriate differences these conditions produce. In fact, unless the social project is conceived with universal scope it cannot both protect and promote these differences. In an important sense, the religious dimension of Kant's ethics supports the deep structure of the moral project. For Kant moral faith defines true religion, and he projects that the ecumenical spirit within "true religion" will transform particular historical religions into genuine ethical communities. In the *Religion* Kant tells us of this hope: "We have good reason to say, however, that 'the kingdom of God is come unto us' once the principle of the gradual transition of ecclesiastical faith to the universal religion of reason, and so to a (divine) ethical state on earth, has become general and has also gained somewhere a *public* foothold, even though the actual establishment of this state is still infinitely removed from us."[11]

Ecumenicalism mirrors the cosmopolitan condition that Kant maintains is the ultimate goal of cultural development. Kant thus anticipates a form of cultural development that will absorb social movements articulated on the basis of cultural, political, and economic goals into a genuinely ecumenical ethical community.

Where does this leave the duties of ordinary persons? I have argued that moral duties to promote the highest good are specified in relation to the achievement of the historical goals that instantiate this ideal. Citizens of democratic societies have obligations to maintain and promote just institutions both within their states and through the expression of public opinion to shape the strategic aims of their nation in relation to other states. Through their voluntary associations, individuals also have obligations to work cooperatively with the citizens of other nations to formulate solutions to common problems. Democratic societies must become the locus of a cosmopolitan public concerned with human rights and human welfare. Economic institutions must also be shaped in keeping with these objectives. This requires the formulation of an ecological model of economic sustainability that can incorporate the improvement of developing nations and future generations. Such a framework is emerging out of consideration for the sustainability of natural resources, for the integrity of the environment, and for the survival and welfare of nonhuman species in the context of continuing economic development. These are not merely pragmatic concerns necessary for the more efficient achievement of material goods, but grow out of the requirements of a just order. In fact the continuation of an instrumentalist attitude toward future development can only frustrate the achievement of these goals. Through a combination of commitment to these goals and a critical and reflective analysis of the limitations of our traditional frameworks, a deeper understanding can be expected to emerge.

Emergent problems are thus extremely complex, conceptually as well as in terms of their material magnitude and scale. They cannot be addressed by national policy alone. Their solutions require international cooperation on a new basis. National interest, even the interest in trade and security, will not be sufficient. Citizens must define their interests in cosmopolitan terms in order to transcend the limitations inherent to the politics of national interest. Ordinary citizens, then, have an extremely important role to play in the emergence of a global society and a global politics. This "unwritten code," the principles formulated by ethical communities and articulated by cosmopolitan public opinion, must shape international law in such a manner as to enable the federation, as the "negative substitute" for legal coercion, to positively maintain a peaceable world order. Moral life will become increasingly challenging.

Notes

Introduction: Brief History of the Criticism of Moral Progress in History

1. Emil Fackenheim, "Kant's Concept of History," in *The God Within: Kant, Schelling, and Historicity*, edited by John Burbidge (Toronto: University of Toronto Press, 1996), p. 48; reprinted from *Kantstudien* 58, no. 3 (1956–57): 381–98.

2. Paul Stern, "The Problem of History and Temporality in Kantian Ethics," *Review of Metaphysics* 39 (1986).

3. William Galston, *Kant and the Problem of History* (Chicago: University of Chicago Press, 1975).

4. Immanuel Kant, "An Old Question Raised Again: Is the Human Race Constantly Progressing?" translated by Robert E. Anchor, in *On History*, edited by Lewis White Beck (New York: Macmillan, 1963), p. 144.

5. Ibid., p. 142.

6. Immanuel Kant, "Idea for a Universal History from a Cosmopolitan Point of View," translated by Lewis White Beck, in *On History*, ed. Beck, p. 15.

7. Yirmiahu Yovel, *Kant and the Philosophy of History* (Princeton: Princeton University Press, 1980). After many decades of criticism, Yovel's book made Kant's philosophy of history respectable again by demonstrating the historical significance of the highest good. However, Yovel maintains that the writings on history are restricted in their significance to political (not moral) progress. His views on the "history of reason" are drawn from the *Critiques* and the *Religion*.

8. Paul Guyer, "Nature, Morality and the Possibility of Peace," in *Proceedings of the Eighth International Kant Congress*, edited by Hoke Robinson (Milwaukee, Wisc.: Marquette University Press, 1995), vol. 1, pt. 1, pp. 51–69.

9. Sharon Anderson–Gold, "Kant's Ethical Commonwealth: The Highest Good as a Social Goal," *International Philosophical Quarterly*, March 1986; also Allen Wood, *Kant's Moral Religion* (Ithaca: Cornell University Press, 1970). While not

stressing the social conditions as fundamentally as I do, Wood calls attention to evil as implicit in the human condition.

10.   Immanuel Kant, "Conjectural Beginning of Human History," translated by Emil L. Fackenheim, in *On History*, ed. Beck, p. 60.

11.   Gerald Barnes, "In Defense of Kant's Doctrine of the Highest Good," *Philosophical Forum*, n.s., 2 (1971).

12.   Pauline Kleingeld, "Kant, History, and the Idea of Moral Development," *History of Philosophy Quarterly* 16, no. 1 (January 1999). Kleingeld reviews and dismisses certain forms of the incompatibility thesis, particularly as formulated by Fackenheim and Despland. She maintains quite correctly that these charges are not of merely historical interest but could "jeopardize the coherence" of Kant's moral theory (p. 59).

13.   Lewis White Beck, *A Commentary on Kant's Critique of Practical Reason* (Chicago: University of Chicago Press, 1960), pp. 244–45. Beck argues that the highest good is not really a practical concept but a dialectical ideal of reason required by Kant's architectonic purpose of uniting the two legislations of reason.

14.   John Silber, "Kant's Concept of the Highest Good as Immanent and Transcendent," *Philosophical Review* 68 (October 1956).

15.   Thomas Auxter, "The Unimportance of Kant's Highest Good," *Journal of the History of Philosophy* (April 1979).

16.   Thomas Auxter, *Kant's Moral Teleology* (Macon, Ga.: Mercer University Press, 1982), chap. 6. Auxter argues that there is no moral warrant for the requirement that (physical) happiness be exactly proportioned to virtue. In addition to the fact that physical happiness is irrelevant to the true rewards of virtue, denying such physical contentment to those who are not virtuous may further inhibit their capacity to become virtuous. Auxter maintains that our primary concern with the physical conditions of life should be to use them to enhance our autonomy and through this our capacity for morality. I sympathize with Auxter's analysis of the "true rewards" of virtue. Furthermore, our inability to directly judge the virtue of others makes any retributionism on the part of human actors morally problematic and therefore inappropriate to any duty to promote the highest good.

17.   Pauline Kleingeld, "What Do the Virtuous Hope For?: Re-reading Kant's Doctrine of the Highest Good," in *Proceedings of the Eighth International Kant Congress*, ed. Robinson, vol. 1, pt. 1, p. 107.

18.   Ibid., p. 109.

19.   Anderson–Gold, "Kant's Ethical Commonwealth."

20.   Immanuel Kant, *Religion within the Limits of Reason Alone*, translated by Theodore M. Greene and Hoyt H. Hudson (New York: Harper & Brothers, 1960), bk. 3.

21.   Kant, "An Old Question Raised Again," trans. Anchor, p. 142. Here Kant ascribes to the species a "limited good will." This good will, entailed by Kant's notion of an innate and incorruptible predisposition to the good, would appear to be the equivalent of an individual's disposition in providing the point of reference against which to judge the empirical character of the species.

22.   Kleingeld, "Kant, History, and the Idea of Moral Development." Kleingeld argues that while Kant's view of the universality and a temporality of human

consciousness of the moral law salvages the moral equality thesis, moral development generates another kind of historical inequality between generations—namely, it creates a sense of greater blameworthiness of earlier generations for their lesser degree of moral progress. Kleingeld considers the claim that this is "unfair" and maintains that it is not provided that earlier generations could have known better. This entails a complicated debate concerning the moral significance of certain forms of "cultural knowledge" but in principle I agree with Kleingeld's point. In "Perpetual Peace," Kant maintained that fewer impediments to virtue also increase "culpability" for transgressions. That would seem to even the score. I would also add that with fewer impediments, the opportunities to promote the highest good increase and so do one's moral obligations, making the moral life perhaps more challenging for later generations. In any case, how the individual stands in relation to the condition of the species is not a straightforward matter, and this at least leaves room for saints and heroines.

23. Kant, *Religion within the Limits of Reason Alone*, trans. Greene and Hudson, p. 27. "He is evil by nature, means but this, that evil can be predicated of man as a species; not that such a quality can be inferred from the concept of his species (that is, of man in general)—for then it would be necessary" (p. 27).

24 Ibid., pp. 21–23. Kant also calls these predispositions "original" because they are bound up with the possibility of human nature and cannot be eliminated or extirpated. So not only is the "concept of man" free of evil but so too is human nature at its basic or "intelligible" level. Evil may pertain to the intelligible disposition of an individual and to the sensible appearance of the species, but it would appear that there can be no equivalent of the bad will at the level of the species.

Chapter 1. Purposiveness and Cognition

1. John Zammito, *The Genesis of Kant's Critique of Judgment* (Chicago: University of Chicago Press, 1992); Ruldolf Makkreel, *Imagination and Interpretation in Kant: The Hermeneutical Import of the Critique of Judgment* (Chicago: University of Chicago Press, 1990).

2. Zammito, *Genesis of Kant's Critique of Judgment*, pp. 292–93.

3. Immanuel Kant, *Critique of Practical Reason*, translated by Lewis White Beck ((New York: Bobbs–Merrill, 1956), p. 9 n. 7. Kant defines life and pleasure in fundamentally transcendental terms. "Life is the faculty of a being by which it acts according to the laws of the faculty of desire. . . . Pleasure is the idea of the agreement of an object or an action with the subjective conditions of life, i.e., with the faculty through which an idea causes the reality of its object." Through these definitions the faculty of feeling is brought into relation with the faculty of desire, or *Willkur*.

4. Makkreel, *Imagination and Interpretation in Kant*, pp. 88, 156.

5. Beck, *Commentary on Kant's Critique of Practical Reason*, pp. 244–45.

6. Kant, "Idea for a Universal History," trans. Beck, p. 11.

7. Ibid.

8. Immanuel Kant, *Critique of Judgment*, translated by J. H. Bernard (New York: Hafner Press, 1974), introduction, p.22.

9. Makkreel, *Imagination and Interpretation in Kant*, p. 167.

10. Immanuel Kant, *Critique of Pure Reason*, translated by Norman Kemp Smith (New York: St. Martin's Press, 1965), p. 533.

11. Irmgard Scherer, "Kant's Eschatology in *Zum ewigen Frieden*: The Concept of Purposiveness to Guarantee Perpetual Peace," in *Proceedings of the Eighth International Kant Congress*, ed. Robinson, vol. 2, pt. 1, p. 441.

12. Kant, *Critique of Judgment*, trans. Bernard, p. 220.

13. Ibid., p. 220.

14. Unless God is reintroduced on independent grounds, the system of purposiveness must terminate in man. But God's existence is not given. God's existence in the Critical System is postulated on moral grounds that are themselves given in and through man's existence.

15. Kant, *Critique of Judgment*, trans. Bernard, pp. 293–94.

16. Makkreel, *Imagination and Interpretation in Kant*, pp. 137–38.

17. Ibid., p. 137.

18. This first level may be what Makkreel means by "descriptions of natural and historical processes" (ibid., p. 137). I want to emphasize here the phenomenological aspect of what is taken to be a "sign."

19. Makkreel, *Imagination and Interpretation in Kant*, p. 151. Makkreel argues that the use of the French Revolution as a historical sign has a double function. It intimates a better future by serving as the imaginative projection of the teleological ideas of the federation and the cosmopolitan society, but it also authenticates this interpretation by serving as a confirmation of the moral predisposition that will bring these ideals to reality. Reflective teleological and determinate practical judgments intersect in the authentic interpretation of historical signs, making a *wahrsagende*, or prophetic, history possible.

20. Hannah Ginsborg, "Purposiveness and Normativity," in *Proceedings of the Eighth International Kant Congress*, ed. Robinson, vol. 2, pt. 1, pp. 453–59. Ginsborg provides an interesting analysis of the normativity of different types of judgments. She argues that the connection between purposiveness and normativity has been underappreciated and that it is this connection that can provide a univocal meaning for the different contexts of teleological judgment.

21. There is an extensive literature that regards the inclusion of happiness in the necessary object of the moral law as heteronomy because happiness is derived from our material desires. For a good review of the controversies surrounding the role of happiness in Kant's ethics, see Victoria Wike, *Kant on Happiness in Ethics* (New York: State University of New York Press, 1994). However, since the happiness aimed at is that which is due the worthy, it can be argued that the desires of the worthy would be morally informed. The fulfillment of morally informed desires seems not only appropriate but an extension of the respect due humanity as a moral species which qua humanity has a natural component.

22. Auxter, *Kant's Moral Teleology*. Strictly speaking, as noted earlier, Auxter rejects the idea of an obligation to promote the highest good insofar as this is

defined in terms of an exact proportion of virtue and *physical happiness*. Instead, he argues for the centrality of the idea of an ectypal world to guide the construction of a moral teleology and for an enriched understanding of the intrinsic rewards of a life of virtue pursued in cooperation with others.

23. Ibid., p. 181.

24. Kant, *Religion within the Limits of Reason Alone*, trans. Greene and Hudson. "But that everyone ought to make the highest good possible in the world a final end is a synthetic practical proposition a priori. . . . This extension is possible because of the moral law's being taken in relation to the natural characteristic of man, that for all his actions he must conceive of an end over and above the law . . ." (preface, p. 7nn).

25. Gordon Michalson Jr., *Fallen Freedom: Kant on Radical Evil and Moral Regeneration* (Cambridge: Cambridge University Press, 1990). Although critical of the success of the Kantian project, which Michalson views as no longer meaningful for our times, this book-length study offering insights into the complexity of the Kantian conception of moral evil is an exception to the general neglect of this topic.

Chapter 2. From Autonomy to Radical Evil: The Social Context of Virtue and Vice

1. Emil Fackenheim, "Kant and Radical Evil," in *God Within*, ed. Burbidge, p. 21; reprinted from *University of Toronto Quarterly* 22 (1953): 339–53.

2. Immanuel Kant, "What is Enlightenment?" translated by Lewis White Beck, in *On History*, ed. Beck, p. 3.

3. Immanuel Kant, *Groundwork of the Metaphysics of Morals*, translated by H. J. Paton (New York: Harper and Row, 1956). "The concept of the intelligible world is thus only *a point of view* which reason finds itself constrained to adopt outside appearances *in order to conceive itself as practical*" (p. 126).

4. Immanuel Kant, *The Metaphysical Principles of Virtue*, translated by James Ellington (Indianapolis, Ind.: Bobbs–Merrill, 1964), p. 26. In this passage Kant explains that freedom of choice is a characteristic of *Willkur*, or the faculty of desire broadly defined. Choice is not an attribute of *Wille*, or pure practical reason, because this is the source of the moral law. Nonetheless, the moral law is a condition of autonomy and hence ultimately of freedom. As Kant elaborated the relation of the will to desire, to maxims, and to the phenomenal world, he not only articulated the distinction between *Wille* and *Willkur*, but, in the *Religion*, introduced concepts required to locate moral evil—disposition, propensity, predisposition, etc.—that ultimately specify the moral character of the will. When I refer to practical freedom in its historical manifestations, I am referring to *Willkur*.

5. Kant, *Groundwork of the Metaphysics of Morals*, trans. Paton. "Will is a kind of causality belonging to living beings so far as they are rational. Freedom would then be the property this causality has of being able to work independently of determination by alien causes . . ." (p. 114).

6. Kant, *Religion within the Limits of Reason Alone*, trans. Greene and Hudson. "An objective end (i.e., the end we ought to have) is that which is proposed to us as such by reason alone" (p. 6n).

7. Ibid.

8. Ibid, pp. 4, 6n. "For in the absence of all reference to an end no determination of the will can take place in man" and "And yet it is one of the inescapable limitations of man and of his faculty of practical reason . . . to have regard in every action, to the consequence thereof, in order to discover what could serve him as an end. . . ."

9. Kant, *Critique of Practical Reason*, trans. Beck. "The faculty of desire is the faculty such a being has of causing, through its ideas, the reality of the objects of these ideas" (p. 9n).

10. Ibid., p. 72.

11. Kant, *Groundwork of the Metaphysics of Morals*, trans. Paton, p. 101.

12. Auxter, *Kant's Moral Teleology*. Auxter argues that the English translation of *Verbindlichkeit* as obligation in terms of constraint tends to miss the positive connotations that it carries in Kant's German usage. "Yet the meaning of *Verbindlichkeit* is not restricted to this idea of constraint. . . . Here the meaning of 'bound' is positive: we are united with others and hence bound up with them" (p. 164).

13. One such consideration is the question whether the unworthy are in some sense to be denied happiness, even if the happiness they seek is not immoral or is morally neutral.

14. As I noted earlier, Auxter rejects the obligation to promote the highest good. He also takes note of our epistemological limitations, but his rejection goes to the retributivist conception underlying its allocation. He argues that improving the physical conditions (happiness) of an immoral agent may improve the capacity for morality and that our obligations to others should be guided by the ideal of developing the conditions of autonomous choice in all agents. When the concept of the highest good is set in the context of the propensity to evil, which requires a united ethical community, it becomes clearer that we are not in a moral position to carry out the retributivist agenda. Law, on the other hand, may have a retributivist character, but that has a different derivation and justification.

Chapter 3. Radical Evil and the Ethical Commonwealth

1. Kant, *Religion within the Limits of Reason Alone*, trans. Greene and Hudson, p. 18n. Kant's view that evil is an active impediment is derived from his claim that the moral law is a *motivating force*. Because reason is practical in this strong sense, absence of agreement with the moral law is only possible on the assumption of an opposing incentive. Were there not an opposing incentive, the will would automatically agree with the moral law, and the will would be "holy." Apparently the moral law would not appear as an incentive in the sense of a constraint for a holy will. But in fact, Kant argues, the moral law is given to us as an incentive with which the will is not automatically in accord;

therefore, we can also infer that our will contains a ground of opposition. We don't need evil deeds to arrive at this conclusion.

2. Ibid., p. 46.

3. Michalson, *Fallen Freedom*, p. 38.

4. Kant, *Religion within the Limits of Reason Alone*, trans. Greene and Hudson, p. 21.

5. Ibid., p. 28.

6. Michalson, *Fallen Freedom*, p. 38.

7. Ibid., p. 22.

8. It may be objected that this analysis leaves the predisposition to animality entirely out of the picture as a predisposition that can be deliberately misused and so be a source of moral vice. I believe that this can be explained by interpreting the vices that stem from an abuse/misuse of the sexual impulses as first and foremost objectifications of the self (under the corrupted principle of self-love) as an instrument of pleasure. The teleological dimensions of this predisposition must first be reflectively interpreted through a concept of duties to ourselves in order to become denigrations of our "humanity." This would leave the real location of the propensity to evil in the corruption of the predisposition to humanity.

9. Michalson, *Fallen Freedom*. Although Michalson recognizes the important relationship between the predispositions and evil, he connects evil more closely with the body than I do. He says: "The universality of radical evil is thus connected with the givenness of the body" (p. 69). He also has little to say about the role of the ethical commonwealth in individual moral development, treating this task as a more individual endeavor. He refers to Kant's remarks on this topic as "tentative," suggesting that he does not regard this ideal as particularly important for an interpretative study of moral evil. He says: "Moreover, Kant's own tentative remarks about what he calls an ethical commonwealth suggest the hint of a link between his largely privatized theory of autonomy and a more historicized, social conception of purposeful human activity, as we find in Marx" (p. 130). My analysis of the relationship between books 1 and 3 of the *Religion* reveals a strong connection between moral evil and the ethical commonwealth, and such a connection illumines much about the notions of moral progress in history that are found in Kant's essays on history.

10. Kant, *Religion within the Limits of Reason Alone*, trans. Greene and Hudson, p. 29.

11. Kant, *Metaphysical Principles of Virtue*, trans. Ellington, p. 26.

12. Kant, *Religion within the Limits of Reason Alone*, trans. Greene and Hudson, p. 18n.

13. Wood, *Kant's Moral Religion*, p. 219.

14. Kant, *Religion within the Limits of Reason Alone*, trans. Greene and Hudson, p. 31.

15. Ibid., p. 46.

16. Ibid., p. 85.

17. Ibid., p. 22.

18. Ibid., p. 88.

19. Ibid., pp. 85–86.

20. Kant, *Groundwork of the Metaphysics of Morals*, trans. Paton, p. 101.

21. Ibid.

22. Kant, *Religion within the Limits of Reason Alone*, trans. Greene and Hudson, p. 88.

23. Kant, *Groundwork of the Metaphysics of Morals*, trans. Paton, p. 101.

24. Kant, *Religion within the Limits of Reason Alone*, trans. Greene and Hudson, p. 89.

25. Ibid., p. 89.

26. Ibid., p. 89.

27. Philip Rossi, S.J., "Evil and the Moral Power of God," in *Proceedings of the Sixth International Kant Congress* (Lanham, Md.: Center for Advanced Research in Phenomenology and University Press of America, 1989), vol. 2, pt. 2, p. 376.

28. Kant, *Religion within the Limits of Reason Alone*, trans. Greene and Hudson, p. 88.

29. Philip Rossi, S.J., "Autonomy and Community: The Social Character of Kant's Moral Faith," *Modern Schoolman* 61 (1984): 185.

30. Ibid.

31. While the predisposition to personality guarantees that we cannot lose our receptivity to the moral law, this alone cannot ground a collective undertaking such as the ethical commonwealth because it cannot provide for the coordination that the constitution or design of the ethical commonwealth is meant to introduce into our collective efforts.

32. Clement Webb, *Kant's Philosophy of Religion* (Oxford: Oxford University Press, 1926; reprint, New York: Kraus Reprint Co., 1970), pp. 198, 191.

33. Michalson, *Fallen Freedom,*: p. 126.

34. Martin Buber, *I And Thou*, translated by Ronald Gregor Smith, 2d ed. (New York: Charles Scribner's Sons, 1958). The issue of the constancy of moral commitment also figures into Buber's analysis. The human capacity to enter into I–Thou relationships is inconstant and threatened by social–cultural conflicts resulting in human objectification. God's enduring presence as a Thou provides the ground of the possibility of the renewal of spiritual and ethical relationships.

35. Immanuel Kant, "What is Orientation in Thinking?" in *Kant: Political Writings*, translated by H. B. Nisbet, edited by Hans Reiss (Cambridge: Cambridge University Press, 1991).

36. Harry Van der Linden, *Kantian Ethics and Socialism* (Indianapolis, Ind.: Hackett, 1988).

Chapter 4. Cultural Differentiation: The Origins of History

1. Kant, "Idea for a Universal History," trans. Beck, p. 12.

2. Ibid., p. 13.

3. Allen Wood, "Kant's Historical Materialism," in *Autonomy and Community: Kant's Social Philosophy Today*, edited by Sidney Axnin and Jane Kneller (Albany: State University of New York Press, 1998), p. 22.

4. Richard Velkley, *Freedom and the End of Reason* (Chicago: University of Chicago Press, 1989), p. 13.

5. Kant, "Idea for a Universal History," trans. Beck, p. 21.

6. Kant, "Conjectural Beginning of Human History," trans. Fackenheim, p. 56. Speaking of the first step into freedom, Kant writes: "He discovered in himself a power of choosing for himself a way of life, of not being bound without alternative to a single way, like the animals." Differences in human "ways of life" or cultures are prefigured in the beginnings of human freedom.

7. Ibid., p. 53.

8. Ibid., p. 58.

9. Ibid., p. 63.

10. The power of practical reason may be complete from the beginning, but the full power of speculative reason clearly is not. Since speculative reason plays a role in the adequacy of the conceptualizations underlying moral judgments, there is a sense in which moral judgments derived from inadequate concepts can be inadequate or immature. The duty to perfect reason in all its powers underlies the duty of enlightenment, which is nonetheless a duty that can be pursued only in a social context. Immaturity, while a stage in the development of moral evil, is not itself a culpable condition. And the species is, of course, not a moral agent. Nonetheless, the cultural condition of the species is, I believe, a relevant factor in determining the degree of culpability for individuals. This will become clearer in the course of my arguments.

11. Kant, "Conjectural Beginning of Human History," trans. Fackenheim, p. 67. Without the full development of culture, reason cannot come to maturity and the highest good within which this tension is resolved cannot be achieved. The moral good, as I have argued, is not a merely individual good but is the fulfillment of a telos that entails the perfection of both the individual and the species. Even if in a primitive condition somehow all individuals were to suddenly become morally good simultaneously, the highest good would not be achieved, because the species would not have attained the complete perfection for which it is destined. This is the basis of Galston's complaint that Kant's philosophy of history treats individuals as means to the ends of the species. However, the highest good is morally binding on individuals, so it is perhaps more to the point to complain that the highest good treats individuals as means or at least may require some sacrifice of individual happiness. At any rate, the criticism is miscast. The problem is that the traditional complaint treats Kant's conceptions of good and evil as if they were inherently individualistic. If it were not for the fact that Kant's most basic moral characterizations of good and evil are intrinsically social, this traditional complaint might have some merit.

12. Ibid., p. 61.

13. Ibid., p. 62.

14. Ibid., p. 68.

15. Ibid.

16. Kant, *Religion within the Limits of Reason Alone*, trans. Greene and Hudson, p 22.

Chapter 5. Purposiveness and Political Progress

1. That this task is unavoidable in a practical as well as a moral sense is indicated for Kant by the finitude of the physical world or "globe." Justice receives its structure from these limits.

2. Immanuel Kant, "On the Common Saying: 'This may be true in theory but it does not apply to practice,'" in *Kant: Political Writings*, ed. Reiss, translated by H. B. Nisbet. In this essay Kant makes the following interesting statement concerning his own position within the historical order: "I am a member of a series of human generations, and as such, I am not as good as I ought to be or could be according to the moral requirements of my nature" (p. 88).

3. In addition to the practical problems involved in trying to render aid to the citizens of nations hostile to our own, the cut between what is required by charity and what is due because of justice depends upon settling conflicting claims, not only to territory but also to resources that have been developed through force or fraud. In "Perpetual Peace" in the section on the law of world citizenship, Kant, despite his general approval of commerce, clearly condemns the commercial activities that led to the exploitation of the Sugar Islands and goes so far as to praise the prudence of China and Japan in restricting the economic interactions of their people with the West.

4. Kant, "Idea for a Universal History," trans. Beck, pp. 25–26.

5. Kant, "An Old Question Raised Again," trans. Anchor, p. 137.

6. Ibid., p. 147.

7. Ibid., p. 143.

8. Makkreel, *Imagination and Interpretation in Kant*, p. 153. Makkreel's study of the role of the imagination in reflective judgment makes an important contribution to understanding the status of Kant's philosophy of history. He explains the important interplay between reflective interpretative judgment and teleological determinant judgment in Kant's theory of signs. Quoting the *Anthropology*, Makkreel explains that signs are an extension of the imagination's ability to utilize the present as a means of connecting representations of projected future events with those of past events. "The imagination is obviously important in such an interpretation, since any past event or future goal is by nature not directly intuitable. " I also noted in my article "Kant's Ethical Anthropology," *History of Philosophy Quarterly* 11, no. 4 (1994): 405–19, the manner in which such judgments appear to project a future goal onto the past so as to resignify the meaning of the past event for the "sympathetic spectator." At that time I had not fully appreciated the reflective character of the judgment and the role of imagination in its construction.

9. Kant, "An Old Question Raised Again," trans. Anchor, p. 148.

10. Kant, *Religion within the Limits of Reason Alone*, trans. Greene and Hudson, p. 23.

11. This breaks the parallel between the individual and the species, but not the interdependence. The species does not, strictly speaking, have a "disposition." The character of the species is evil because individuals (whose dispositions must be either good or evil) freely choose evil. But the predisposition

to the good remains active in the species and so constitutes a resource for even the individual of bad character to draw upon.

12. Michalson, *Fallen Freedom*, p. 64. Michalson provides an excellent analysis of the specific meanings and distinctions between predispositions, propensities, nature, and freedom.

13. Kant, *Religion within the Limits of Reason Alone*, trans. Greene and Hudson, p. 26. Here Kant distinguishes between two senses of "act" in the exercise of freedom, both of which are attributable to *Willkur*. In the first sense, which pertains to the propensity to evil, the act is a timeless formal ground of all further particular acts. Particular actions, which are temporal, are acts in the second derivative sense. Even *Willkur*, then, has a timeless or intelligible character.

14. Sharon Anderson–Gold, "Kant's Rejection of Devilishness: The Limits of Human Volition," *Idealistic Studies* 14 (1984).

15. Kant, "Conjectural Beginning of Human History," trans. Fackenheim, p. 60.

16. The ethical commonwealth, like the true republic, is a kind of regulative ideal for historical development. Ethical communities, like republican governments, are then historical approximations of these ideals.

17. It is interesting that Kant's statement that the "profit" is in the products of legality has often been taken in a pessimistic manner to mean that moral improvement is not a consequence of historical striving. In this paragraph Kant notes that we must rely upon empirical data to indicate "the moral state of the human race," because we are limited to phenomena. That is, of course, a consequence of Kantian epistemology and applies equally well to individual judgments concerning right action and morally good character. But I do not take this paragraph to be denying historical moral improvement. Quite the contrary, Kant uses moral qualifiers throughout the passage.

18. This spontaneity is what enables reason to critique itself, to orient itself in relation to nature, to acquire knowledge of the principles of experience and the principles of morality, and ultimately to settle metaphysical disputes concerning man's place in the cosmos.

19. Immanuel Kant, *Metaphysical Elements of Justice*, translated by John Ladd (New York: Bobbs–Merrill, 1965), p. 76.

20. Makkreel, *Imagination and Interpretation in Kant*, p. 153.

21. Sympathy in this context would seem to be unlike the pathological emotion of sympathetic response to pain or suffering, an emotion Kant did not approve of.

22. Makkreel, *Imagination and Interpretation in Kant*, p. 158.

23. Ibid., pp. 170–71. Makkreel explains that the inclusion of the interpreting subject in the grounding of the human sciences need not lead to subjectivism. "This is because direct discriminatory judgments using aesthetic and teleological orientation contribute to the process of finding our place within the overall horizon of the life–world. . . . Ultimately the detailed knowledge obtained in the human sciences through such analysis must be related back to the original life–world."

24. Hannah Arendt, *Lectures on Kant's Political Philosophy*, edited by Ronald Beiner (Chicago: University of Chicago Press, 1982).

25. Ibid., p. 77.

26. Cited by Ronald Beiner in his "Interpretive Essay" in ibid., p. 126.

27. Stern, "Problem of History and Temporality in Kantian Ethics," and Galston, *Kant and the Problem of History*, also express just such a concern about the strange ontological status of the "species" in Kant's philosophy of history.

28. The conception of a continuous humanity is needed to provide the vehicle of identification with an indefinite future. It is here that Kant's notion of religious–ethical community helps to fill in the frame. Unlike specific political and cultural traditions that can develop but must remain particular, the ethical commonwealth, based on our common humanity, is universal. Because Kant's ethical commonwealth is fully universal, it can encompass the indefinite future while providing continuity through time with specific historical faiths grounded in particular cultures.

29. Van der Linden, *Kantian Ethics and Socialism*.

30. I am not claiming that the species is itself an agent with a moral disposition. Rather I am working out the implications of Kant's anthropology, which endows each person with an ineradicable moral predisposition and a propensity to evil that inheres in our social inclinations. The propensity to evil corrupts the development of cultural and social institutions, while the moral predisposition ensures that human beings will, despite such corruptions, continue to recognize and respond to conditions that support institutional reform. Thus we come to judge our own social/cultural creations according to ethical criteria and attempt to shape them to provide a better "fit" with moral ideals.

31. Immanuel Kant, *Logic*, translated by Robert Hartman and Wolfgang Schwartz (Indianapolis, Ind.: Bobbs–Merrill, 1974), p. 94.

32. Kant, "Idea for a Universal History," trans. Beck, p. 11. Kant begins this essay by leaving open the metaphysical status of freedom of the will and noting that despite the seeming arbitrariness of freedom, regular patterns in human actions can be discovered if we attend to the "play of freedom of the human will in the large"—that is if we look beyond particular actions to large numbers of actions. Human action as a phenomenon does not fit the strictly causal laws of physics and can be subsumed under "laws" only in the statistical sense.

33. Kant, "On the Common Saying," pp. 88–89.

34. Ibid., p. 89.

35. Perhaps this is a somewhat ambiguous formulation. I believe Kant means that a human being cannot be said to freely choose to reject the moral incentive, so that if, *contra hypothesi*, a "human being" exists without this incentive, such a being is not truly a "human person."

36. Van der Linden, *Kantian Ethics and Socialism*. Nonetheless, it is questionable, as Van der Linden argues, that "intelligent devils" could create a state of perfect justice utilizing only principles of self-interest. In an insightful critique, he points out that Rawls's theory of justice, based on minimal assumptions about the nature of human motivations, in effect morally constrains the choosers in ways similar to the Kantian conception of a moral incentive by means of the "veil of ignorance" and the equalities built into the "original position."

37. Ibid. It may seem that the kind of moral knowledge that we gain from an analysis of the perspective of the spectator is merely passive knowledge that provides no link to action. Van der Linden's interpretation opens the door to action by linking our understanding of what types of purposes fit a moral world with the concept of a commitment over time to promote these purposes.

38. John E. Atwell, *Ends and Principles in Kant's Moral Thought* (Dordrecht: Martinus Nijhoff, 1986).

39. Kant, "An Old Question Raised Again," trans. Anchor, p. 142.

40. In fact, it would seem to have to work this way. Per hypothesis, we are all morally evil and can only become morally good through a moral revolution. This "revolution" within the disposition cannot itself appear in time. When it occurs it breaks the hold of merely prudential reasoning and allows for the dominance of the moral incentive without necessarily introducing a radical break in the phenomena. The "mode of thought" changes, but the empirical character of the agent/actions merely evolves. Moral progress in the political realm, then, is associated with fundamental changes in the way that the public reasons about justice. An interesting corollary of fundamental change is that while we can adjust our judgments concerning the culpability of past agents to their differing conditions, we cannot reverse or relativize our conception of what is right.

41. Kant, "What is Enlightenment?" trans. Beck, pp. 4–5. In discussing the differences between the public and private uses of reason, Kant makes reference to the possibility that on some occasions the individual will take the point of view of "a society of world citizens." Thus, the appropriate public can be extended across national boundaries as well as across time.

42. Kant, "Idea for a Universal History," trans. Beck, p. 24 n. 7.

43. I use the concept of history here in a generic sense that includes Kant's own "universal history" but that could be extended beyond the specific principles of the essay bearing that title. Particular histories are the "records of the historians" in the narrow sense. They may or may not have explicit moral structures, but they are the materials for generic history, which must have a moral structure.

44. Yovel, *Kant and the Philosophy of History*.

45. Kant, "An Old Question Raised Again," trans. Anchor, p. 147.

Chapter 6. Cosmopolitan Publics, International Law, and Human Rights

1. Kant, "Idea for a Universal History," trans. Beck, p. 23.

2. Kant, "Conjectural Beginning of Human History," trans. Fackenheim, p. 65. Cessation of hostilities in the form of an early unification is in this section associated with "the end of liberty," a soulless "despotism," and "culture having barely begun." The moral value of peace, then, is inseparable from issues of law and justice, especially in relation to the just treatment of distinct cultural groups.

3. The cosmopolitan condition was first proclaimed by Kant in the essay

"Idea for a Universal History from a Cosmopolitan Point of View," but the law of world citizenship and the details of the federation of republics were not worked out until the publication of "Perpetual Peace" a decade later. In "Idea for a Universal History" Kant speaks of the cosmopolitan condition as "the womb" of all of mankind's capacities and then foretells the formation of an international government and a "rising . . . feeling . . . for the preservation of the whole" (trans. Beck, p. 23) as events that provide the hope for the cosmopolitan condition to come. In other words, even in this essay Kant views cosmopolitanism as a consequence of a consciously self-preserving international order.

4.   Kant, "Idea for a Universal History," trans. Beck, p. 26.

5.   Immanuel Kant, "Perpetual Peace," translated by Louis White Beck, in *On History*, ed. Beck, p. 105.

6.   Ibid., p. 103.

7.   James Bohman, "The Public Spheres of the World Citizen," in *Proceedings of the Eighth International Kant Congress*, ed. Robinson, vol. 1, pt. 3, pp. 1065–80.

8.   T. M. McCarthy, "Kant's Enlightenment Project Reconsidered," in *Proceedings of the Eighth International Kant Congress*, ed. Robinson, vol. 1, pt. 3, pp. 1049–64.

9.   Kant, "What is Enlightenment?" trans. Beck, p. 5.

10.   Ibid.

11.   Ibid., P. 3.

12.   Ibid., p. 8.

13.   Ibid.

14.   Ibid., p. 7.

15.   Kant, "Idea for a Universal History," trans. Beck, p. 23.

16.   A. J. Milne, *Human Rights and Human Diversity* (Albany: State University of New York Press, 1986).

17.   Ibid.

18.   Anderson-Gold, "Crimes against Humanity: A Kantian Interpretation of International Law," in *Autonomy and Community: Kant's Social Philosophy Today*, edited by Sidney Axnin and Jane Kneller (Albany: State University of New York Press, 1998). See this article for a fuller articulation of my view of the relationship between cultural pluralism and human rights. My positive defense of cultural pluralism owes much to the work of Milne, but my conclusions allowing for limited intervention derive from a different ethical framework for international law.

19.   Kant, "On the Common Saying," p. 75.

20.   Retribution for Kant is a duty of the entire community.

21.   Harry Van der Linden, "Kant: The Duty to Promote International Peace and Political Intervention," in *Proceedings of the Eighth International Kant Congress*, ed. Robinson, vol. 2, pt. 1, pp. 71–79. Van der Linden also argues for a defense of political intervention in terms of the project of perpetual peace. He provides an interesting set of guidelines for when intervention is reasonable in light of this end. While I accept his guidelines, my defense is more directly focused on the concept of right.

22. Kant, *Metaphysical Elements of Justice*, trans. Ladd, p. 76.

23. Although a Kantian federation will require that all members have a republican form of government, this alone does not guarantee substantial equality among citizens or even that all citizens have the same civil rights. It does allow for substantial cultural diversity and for potential conflict over issues of "rights." However, that all who are subject to the law should have a form of legal standing that protects them from arbitrary treatment is, I believe, entailed in Kant's conception of republicanism and can provide the basis for an international intervention in cases of gross violations of basic rights that the contemporary community now terms "crimes against humanity."

24. Anthony Lewis, "A Turn in the Road," *New York Times*, August 1998.

25. Kant, "Perpetual Peace," trans. Beck, p. 150.

26. Arthur Holcombe, *Human Rights in the Modern World* (New York: New York University Press, 1948).

27. Ibid., pp.125–26.

28. Andreas Follesdal, "Global Ethics, Democracy, and Culture," paper presented at the *Fifteenth International Conference on Social Philosophy*, North Adams State University, North Adams, Massachusetts, August 1998.

29. Kant, "Perpetual Peace," trans. Beck, p.134.

30. The work of Jody Williams, coordinator of the International Campaign to Ban Land Mines, is an example of a successful citizen–led political movement. Although the United States did not sign the Oslo treaty to ban land mines, her work has received international attention and led to her winning the Nobel Peace Prize in 1997.

31. Kant, "Idea for a Universal History," trans. Beck, p. 26. Throughout this essay Kant's focus is on the development of a cosmopolitan condition and a federative alliance, not on a strict union of states. The essay presupposes a condition of cultural pluralism and conflict as part of the plan of nature. However, this naturalist perspective is not in competition with, but is a supplement to, Kant's ethical analysis of the value of culture and human responsibility for the evils that arise from social conflict. My interpretation of "radical evil" attempts to show how Kant's concept of the propensity to evil provides an anthropological link between his ethics, theory of culture, and his philosophy of history.

Conclusion: History and the Moral Duties of Individuals

1. While I am primarily concerned to address the issue of apparently increasing degrees of "virtue," it is interesting to note that Freud in his "Civilization and its Discontents" was not sanguine about the relationship between increasing degrees of civilization and happiness. Just as increasing degrees of legality bring greater culpability for transgressions, and greater opportunities to extend moral improvement bring stricter obligations, our increasing degrees of material improvement have psychological consequences that affect our conceptions of happiness.

2. Kant, "An Old Question Raised Again," trans. Anchor, pp. 147–48.

3. Kant, "Perpetual Peace," trans. Beck, p. 128.

4. Kant, "Idea for a Universal History," trans. Beck, p. 23. Kant argues that although funds for civic improvement are wanting due to the investments governments make in military buildups, rulers realize that it is not in their best interests to hinder the internal efforts of their peoples. Since commerce creates a real interdependence between peoples, conflicts between nations will create the need for arbitration and this will prepare the way for a form of international governance that will provide the peace needed for true civic independence. Thus, the goal of civic improvement is tied to the development of a cosmopolitan community.

5. Auxter, *Kant's Moral Teleology*, pp. 175–76.

6. Bohman, "Public Spheres of the World Citizen."

7. Alfred Nordmann, "Community, Immortality, Enlightenment: Kant's Scholarly Republic," in *Proceedings of the Eighth International Kant Congress*, vol. 2, pt. 2, pp. 706–7.

8. Ibid.

9. Philip Rossi, S.J., "The Social Authority of Reason: The 'True Church' as the Locus for Moral Progress," in *Proceedings of the Eighth International Kant Congress*, vol. 2, pt. 2, pp. 679–85. Rossi notes that Kant does not provide a complete account of how such social authority bears upon specific institutions and practices, and that this incompleteness "renders problematic the reliability of efforts to discern the course of moral progress" (p. 681).

10. Ibid., p. 682.

11. Kant, *Religion within the Limits of Reason Alone*, trans. Greene and Hudson, p. 113.

Bibliography

WORKS BY KANT

"Conjectural Beginning of Human History." In *On History*, edited by Lewis White
Beck. New York: Macmillan, 1963.
Critique of Judgment. Translated by J. H. Bernard.
Critique of Practical Reason. Translated by Lewis White Beck. New York: Bobbs–
Merrill, 1956.
Critique of Pure Reason. Translated by Norman Kemp Smith. New York: St. Martin's
Press, 1965.
Groundwork of the Metaphysics of Morals. Translated by H. J. Paton. New York: Harper
and Row, 1956.
"Idea for a Universal History from a Cosmopolitan Point of View." Translated
by Lewis White Beck. In *On History*, edited by Lewis White Beck. New York:
Macmillan, 1963.
The Metaphysical Elements of Justice. Translated by John Ladd. New York: Bobbs–
Merrill, 1965.
The Metaphysical Principles of Virtue. Translated by James Ellington. Indianapolis,
Ind.: Bobbs–Merrill, 1964.
"An Old Question Raised Again: Is the Human Race Constantly Progressing?"
Translated by Robert E. Archer. In *On History*, edited by Lewis White Beck.
New York: Macmillan, 1963.
"On the Common Saying, This may be true in theory but it does not apply in
practice." Translated by H. B. Nisbet. In *Kant: Political Writings*, edited by
Hans Reiss. Cambridge: Cambridge University Press, 1991.
"Perpetual Peace." Translated by Lewis White Beck. In *On History*, edited by Lewis
White Beck. New York: Macmillan, 1963.
Religion within the Limits of Reason Alone. Translated by Theodore M. Greene and
Hoyt H. Hudson. New York: Harper and Brothers, 1960.

"What Is Enlightenment?" Translated by Lewis White Beck. New York: Macmillan, 1963.

"What Is Orientation in Thinking?" In *Kant: Political Writings,* edited by Hans Reiss. Cambridge: Cambridge University Press, 1991.

OTHER WORKS CITED

Anderson–Gold, Sharon. "Crimes against Humanity: A Kantian Interpretation of International Law." In *Autonomy and Community: Kant's Social Philosophy Today,* edited by Sidney Axnin. Albany: State University of New York Press, 1998.

———. "Kant's Ethical Commonwealth: The Highest Good as a Social Goal." *International Philosophical Quarterly,* March 1986.

———. "Kant's Rejection of Devilishness: The Limits of Human Volition." *Idealistic Studies* 14 (1984).

Arendt, Hannah. *Lectures on Kant's Political Philosophy.* Edited by Ronald Beiner. Chicago: University of Chicago Press, 1982.

Atwell, John E. *Ends and Principles in Kant's Moral Thought.* Dordrecht: Martinus Nijhoff, 1986.

Auxter, Thomas. *Kant's Moral Teleology.* Macon, Ga.: Mercer University Press, 1982.

———. "The Unimportance of Kant's Highest Good." *Journal of the History of Philosophy,* April 1979.

Barnes, Gerald. "In Defense of Kant's Doctrine of the Highest Good." *Philosophical Forum,* 1971.

Beck, Lewis White. *A Commentary on Kant's Critique of Practical Reason.* Chicago: University of Chicago Press, 1960.

Bohman, James. "The Public Spheres of the World Citizen." In vol. 1 of *Proceedings of the Eighth International Kant Congress,* edited by H. Robinson. Milwaukee, Wisc.: Marquette University Press, 1995.

Buber, Martin. *I and Thou.* New York: Charles Scribner's Sons, 1958.

Fackenheim, Emil. "Kant and Radical Evil." In *The God Within: Kant, Schelling, and Historicity,* edited by John Burbidge. Toronto: University of Toronto Press, 1996.

———. "Kant's Concept of History." In *The God Within: Kant, Schelling, and Historicity,* edited by John Burbidge. Toronto: University of Toronto Press, 1996.

Follesdale, Andreas. "Global Ethics, Democracy, and Culture." Paper delivered at the Fifteenth International Conference on Social Philosophy, North Adams State University, North Adams, Massachusetts, August 1998.

Galston, William. *Kant and the Problem of History.* Chicago: University of Chicago Press, 1975.

Ginsborg, Hannah. "Purposiveness and Normativity." In vol. 2 of *Proceedings of the Eighth International Kant Congress.,* edited by H. Robinson. Milwaukee, Wisc.: Marquette University Press, 1995.

Guyer, Paul. "Nature, Morality, and the Possibility of Peace." In vol. 1 of *Proceedings of the Eighth International Kant Congress,* edited by H. Robinson. Milwaukee, Wisc.: Marquette University Press, 1995.

Holcombe, Arthur. *Human Rights in the Modern World*. New York: New York University Press, 1948.

Kleingeld, Pauline. "Kant, History, and the Idea of Moral Development." *History of Philosophy Quarterly*, January 1999.

————. "What Do the Virtuous Hope For? Rereading Kant's Doctrine of the Highest Good." In vol. 1 of *Proceedings of the Eighth International Kant Congress*, edited by H. Robinson. Milwaukee, Wisc.: Marquette University Press, 1995.

McCarthy, T. M. "Kant's Enlightenment Project Reconsidered." In vol. 1 of *Proceedings of the Eighth International Kant Congress*, edited by H. Robinson. Milwaukee, Wisc.: Marquette University Press, 1995.

Makreel, Rudolf. *Imagination and Interpretation in Kant: The Hermeneutical Import of the Critique of Judgment*. Chicago: University of Chicago Press, 1990.

Michalson, Gordon, Jr. *Fallen Freedom: Kant on Radical Evil and Moral Regeneration*. Cambridge. Cambridge University Press, 1990.

Milne, A. J. *Human Rights and Human Diversity*. Albany: State University of New York Press, 1986.

Nordmann, Alfred. "Community, Immortality, Enlightenment: Kant's Scholarly Republic." In vol. 2 of *Proceedings of the Eighth International Kant Congress*, edited by H. Robinson. Milwaukee, Wisc.: Marquette University Press, 1995.

Rossi, Philip, S.J. "Autonomy and Community: The Social Character of Kant's Moral Faith." *Modern Schoolman* 61 (1984): 185.

————. "Evil and the Moral Power of God." In vol. 2 of *Proceedings of the Sixth International Kant Congress*, edited by H. Robinson. Lanham, Md.: University Press of America, 1989.

————. "The Social Authority of Reason: The 'True Church' as the Locus for Moral Progress." In vol. 2 of *Proceedings of the Eighth International Kant Congress*, edited by H. Robinson. Milwaukee, Wisc.: Marquette University Press, 1995.

Scherer, Irmagard. "Kant's Eschatology in *Zum ewigen Frieden*: The Concept of Purposiveness to Guarantee Perpetual Peace." In vol. 2 of *Proceedings of the Eighth International Kant Congress*, edited by H. Robinson. Milwaukee, Wisc.: Marquette University Press, 1995.

Silber, John. "Kant's Concept of the Highest Good as Immanent and Transcendent." *Philosophical Review* 68 (October 1956).

Stern, Paul. "The Problem of History and Temporality in Kantian Ethics." *Review of Metaphysics* 39 (1986).

Van der Linden, Harry. "Kant: The Duty to Promote International Peace and Polical Intervention." In vol. 2 of *Proceedings of the Eighth International Kant Congress*, edited by H. Robinson. Milwaukee, Wisc.: Marquette University Press, 1995.

————. *Kantian Ethics and Socialism*. Indianapolis, Ind.: Hackett, 1988.

Velkey, Richard. *Freedom and the End of Reason*. Chicago: University of Chicago Press, 1989.

Webb, Clement. *Kant's Philosophy of Religion*. Oxford: Oxford University Press, 1926.

Wike, Victoria. *Kant on Happiness in Ethics*. New York: State University of New York Press, 1994.

Wood, Allen. "Kant's Historical Materialism." In *Autonomy and Community: Kant's*

Social Philosophy Today, edited by Sidney Axnin. Albany: State University of
    New York Press, 1998.
———. *Kant's Moral Religion.* Ithaca: Cornell University Press, 1970.
Yovel, Yirmiahu. *Kant and the Philosophy of History.* Princeton: Princeton Univer-
    sity Press, 1980.
Zammito, John. *The Genesis of Kant's Critique of Judgment.* Chicago: University of
    Chicago Press, 1992.

Index